SIXTEEN THOUSAND SIX HUNDRED EIGHTY–FIVE SUNRISES

SIXTEEN THOUSAND SIX HUNDRED EIGHTY-FIVE SUNRISES

- Dad Stories -

LEAH AMBLER HAWKINS

ARPress
ILLUMINATING IDEAS.
EMPOWERING VOICES.

ARPress
45 Dan Road Suite 5
Canton MA 02021

Hotline: 1(888) 821-0229
Fax: 1(508) 545-7580

Ordering Information:

Quantity sales. Special discounts are available on quantity purchases by corporations, associations, and others. For details, contact the publisher at the address above.

Printed in the United States of America.

ISBN-13:   Softcover   979-8-89356-098-5
                eBook   979-8-89356-099-2

Library of Congress Control Number: 2024905284

Contents

DEDICATION

To my husband and soulmate Gilbert S. Hawkins Jr. My Dad used to swear up and down. "My daughters will never marry a Hawkins!" He was referring to two of the worst boys in school who lived up in Neersville. Everyone knew of their reputation as troublemakers. In high school Gil, who was newer to the area kept getting called to the principal's office by mistake. I still find it funny I technically "disobeyed" Dad. One of the very few times in my life I disobeyed and did not face dire consequences.

To Dad. In his own endearing way, he gave Gil and me his blessing. Shortly after we first started dating, we were sitting with Dad in the living room. All of a sudden he started shaking his leg vigorously up and down. I asked if he was okay and he said, "I'm fine. I was just picturing bouncing grandkids on my knee." Had Dad lived to see them he would have trotted Christopher, Stephen, Sarah and Kyle and Alex all the way to Boston and Lynn and back and he'd have kept them all safe from falling in too far.

> Trot, trot to Boston.
> Trot, trot to Lynn.
> Look out little one
> Or you'll fall right in.
>
> Trot, trot to Boston.
> Trot, trot to Dover.
> Look out little one
> Or you'll fall right over.

Trot, trot to Boston.
Trot, trot to town.
Look out little one
Or you'll fall right down.

As kids we never knew there was a second or third verse to that rhyme. As soon as we were let go and started dropping in, we'd get hauled back on Dad's lap giggling and exclaiming, "do it again Daddy, do it again."

PREFACE

I remember hearing once an average life span of a human equates to twenty-five thousand sunrises. If you live until you are almost seventy that is about what you get. If you think about it for a moment, twenty-five thousand isn't a lot of anything. It used to be a million of anything seemed an astronomical amount. Now people don't seem to bat an eye over numbers like billions or trillions. To think we as humans only on average get twenty-five thousand or so short days on this earth, it would seem prudent we make each sunrise count. Some folks receive the blessing of enjoying way more. If you reach the century mark it is thirty-six thousand five hundred sunrises give or take leap years.

I did the math on my Dad and even included leap years. He was born on July 15, 1933 and passed away on March 21, 1980. He experienced 16,685 sunrises. I can't help but feel he was somehow short changed. He never saw his daughters or son get married and never hugged his grand kids. Being the father he was it was much more our loss than his. I know God has a reason for all things to happen. Until we meet him we will never understand his wisdom. We simply have to trust God's will.

Feeling Dad was short changed may be a little selfish, but I realize my blessings each and every day I am still on this side of the dirt as they say. I do not intend you to think I am referring to only having the other side of the dirt to look forward to as I was officially born again on June 13, 1976 fully immersed by baptism as Jesus taught us and am looking forward to eternal life with the Father, Son and Holy Ghost and my Dad.

To put this in a different perspective and attempt to relate to you a small part for the reason of this book I know about true sorrow. Yes, I pity myself for not having enough time with Dad. Still, when my best friend Paige and I were little we used to sneak into the old Hillsboro Cemetery adjacent to our property. We had no real business being there and weren't trying to be disrespectful or anything but we walked around and came across a headstone that read, our infant son it breathed and passed away. No other markings of who he was, nothing but that inscription and we couldn't believe what we read. We sat next to him and cried. We realized the pain the parents must have felt knowing they hadn't even had the chance to name him. We talked about what he would have been like and what his name might have been. We even visited him a few times after that so he wouldn't feel lonely. The headstone was not even upright but laying down and we thought of up righting it but lacked the nerve. All we could do was grieve for him. Yet, even then, as little as we were not being well versed in scripture we took heart hoping and knowing this poor innocent was now an angel.

Millions, billions and trillions of atrocities later we have seen on this earth I can't help but know in my heart of hearts by God's grace we will overcome evil. Each of us have special talents and gifts to share on our very short times spent on earth. My Dad spent so little time here but he had unique talents and shared all he could. I hope you enjoy reading a small portion of the happier times we shared with him. Also, just so you know I know dad isn't a proper name but I wish to honor my Dad and my Mom and throughout this book they will be in uppercase.

THE SORTING RITUAL

I usually considered myself lucky to have a baby brother. Little Johnny was seven years younger. Mom would allow us to feed him. I knew I could count on him to be the catalyst for my elaborate plot. He in his highchair and me with baby spoon and little jar of Gerber strained peas in hand would set the stage.

Just as a baby bird learns, he was willing to assist me as I plopped spoonful after spoonful of the slimy green goo in his open mouth. I knew I had to be careful though as I didn't want him spitting any back or worse yet not be able to finish the whole jar. Once the words "all gone," were pronounced and he was suitably wiped down I was set. Step one complete.

Step two took a little more doing. Mom once told me she went to school with members of the little Gerber baby's family. I studied that cute little baby face for a moment or so but, quickly knew my more serious task at hand was to completely scratch that little face off the jar. I scrubbed and scrubbed and resorted to scrape some of the glue residue off with my fingernails. I thought this is going to take forever but, finally I managed to devoid the jar of both goo and glue. Once the jar was washed, rinsed and dried inside and out it was deemed ready and so was I.

Ever so gingerly I caressed my little treasure. It was now my ticket to an adventure. I proceeded to the garage where as I knew he would be Dad was working on a project. Upon showing him my gift, Dad dropped what he was doing and said, "I really need that." "Can I help you Daddy?" "You sure can." he said and then he picked me up with a hug and planted me on the workbench. Just as I knew it would, out came the huge Maxwell House coffee can. He dumped it out in front of me with clinkity, clankity, jingly, jangly noise. After setting out some other jars in my reach and making sure I was all set, I sorted screws, finish nails, wingnuts, washers and whatchamajiggers.

As I think back, I wonder if Dad thought if only to himself, good cheap child labor that keeps her out of trouble. Maybe. All I thought then was I'm helping Daddy. I want to do a good job so he will be proud of me.

The garage completed

SETTING THE TABLE

When my uncouth, roughneck Texas born Dad married Mom, Ramee must have had a hissy fit because her wedding gift to him was Emily Post Book of Etiquette. Many thought she gave it to him out of spite. The more gentile reason I am told, was she knew Dad was going to go into officers training. Regardless of the reason he read every word of it. So many times I heard him say, "My daughters will be raised with grace, poise and dignity."

Our meals were served at the kitchen table. It was up to Dana and me to help Mom set the table. We knew all the basic rules. Fork on the left on top of the napkin, knife and spoon on the right and so on. As probably most families did back then we had a utensil drawer with not one but two or three sets of mixed matched sets of silverware due to attrition or garbage disposal carnage. We would willy nilly grab handfuls of the usual culprits and go about the task at hand. The only thing that confused me sometimes was the knife guideline. It wasn't a steadfast rule you could count on. Someone said the sharp part of the knife should face inwardly. Upon asking why, I was told to avoid injuring the person next to you. Then I was also told it should face away from you to avoid injuring yourself. Being left-handed I struggled with the proper knife and fork usage to begin with and since there was usually only four of us when little Johnny was still in his highchair there seemed to be plenty of room to avoid accidental stabbings.

That guideline, however, did pose a problem for me when we set for company, so I finally decided to just make sure whichever way I decided they all faced the same way. I don't know if Dana ever thought as much about it as I did. Not being much of a vegetable eater she knew the knife was at least useful for hiding your undesirable peas and lima beans.

Even so one major rule was followed without fail. This could not even be considered a guideline. This rule we learned was you did not ever, I repeat ever, even without thinking set Dad's place with mix matched silverware. Just in case you couldn't find a match perhaps due to one still being in the dishwasher you retrieved the offending stray, washed it by hand if necessary and made sure Dad's setting matched. To do otherwise was a fool's errand when you got the lecture, "How many times have I told you?"

"Little missies" practicing grace, poise and dignity.

SETTING THE DINING ROOM TABLE

O n major holidays, setting the table took on a whole new meaning. We had a separate dining room with a formal table, silver cabinet, server and buffet. To get to this usually closed room you could enter from the double doors in the living room or through the butler's pantry down from the kitchen. Dana and I were told in no uncertain terms it was not a playroom. Mom and Dad never really locked the doors to it, but each time we snuck in there to play we were so quiet knowing if we got caught we'd face consequences. We didn't venture in much because it was dark, spooky and mausoleum like. Maybe that's what drew us in there when we were in a mood to scare each other silly.

On special occasions, we had the pleasure of seeing this otherwise neglected room transform. When Dad decided we were ready to handle it, Dana and I were in the kitchen watching and absorbing the aromas of freshly baked pies and turkey with stuffing. Knowing full well what was about to take place, Dad announced, "looks like it is time to set the table." On cue Dana and I yelled, "One, two, three go!" and beat feet through the butler's pantry and struggled a little with the door to the dining room. It stuck sometimes from not being used often. Once inside we made a mad dash for the buffet. Whoever touched it first won. Then came the argument. "That's not fair! You did it last time!" Dad watching all this then said, "Just do it together." Somehow, the victory didn't seem as sweet but we minded. We each took a handle of the huge drawer "One, two, three go!" and pulled.

Since we were only nose height to the top of the drawer all we had to do then was breathe deeply as the smell of camphor wafted over us.

Pardon the pun, but that scent was breathtaking. Since this drawer had remained tightly shut since the last holiday the fumes built up and released directly into our nostrils. Then on tippy toes we peered into the drawer to see the beautiful set of neatly stacked matching real silverware gleaming and untarnished thanks to the marvelous camphor sticks I'm pretty certain had been purchased at Nichols Hardware.

Upon seeing all the extra utensils like salad forks, soup spoons and butter knives and dessert forks I was glad to know even where each of those were to be placed. Later on in life I get a giggle when I watch *Pretty Woman*. She gets help from the hotel manager and then at the restaurant blurts out, "Where's the salad? That's the fork I knew." I can't help but smile remembering those times in the dining room.

CLEARING THE DINING ROOM TABLE

O ther dining room accoutrements which fascinated us were such things as the crisply starched and immaculately kept table linens. When pulled from their drawer you caught a whiff of Niagra Spray Starch. On the pristine white tablecloth we put two silver candleabras. Always nearby was the silver candle snuffer. On the candles we fitted exquisite glass cups called bobeche which caught the dribbling wax. I loved the name bobeche. It sounded elegant and refined. Not only that they served a great purpose which I will relate to in a minute. Another wonder to behold was the crystal knife and fork rests. The ends of these were prisms. Dana and I were transfixed by these items but knew better than to simply grab them. We also knew better than to ask to be excused from the table or we would lose the chance to play our game.

Once Dad officially declared the meal over he didn't have to but he asked if we would like to snuff out the candles. No cupping of the hands or blowing the candles out. That was for birthday cakes. This game took dexterity, finesse and concentration. In turn we were allowed to pick up the snuffer and approach a candle. Dad rated us for best candle snuffing technique. The Olympics of candle snuffing. A perfect ten entailed a snip of the wick about a quarter of an inch above the candle and the least possible amount of smoke involved in the snuffing process. Easy if you are an adult but even then maybe. We were seven or eight years old. This was more nerve wracking than trying to lift the funny bone out of the game of Operation without getting the buzzer. If you really did a poor job of snuffing you would be disqualified and Heaven forbid any wax ended up on the table linen.

Lucky for us most of it landed on the bobeche. Usually if we did poorly, Dad would relight all the candles and let us try again for practice. We couldn't do it too many times though because by then the wicks were too short to snip and that is where you had the most chance of wax blobs on the tablecloth bobeche or not.

Once snuffing was done it was time to move on to consider the knife and fork rests. Gently place the carving knife or fork on a plate NOT on the tablecloth. Pick up the heavy crystal and close one eye. With the other eye you marveled at the refractions and rainbows it held. Sometimes Dad would even relight a candle so we could look at the flame through the prism. All said and done I'm surprised the table ever got cleared.

BEGATS

John Estol Berry Sr. or Pop married Neta Winona Williamson or Gramma. They lived in a tiny town Spur Texas. They begat two children. Dad's older sister Ernestine married E.H. Meadows. E.H. was a teacher and a rancher. Ernestine had a dress shop in Bastrop and she was practically a concert pianist. Gramma taught piano so she Ernestine learned early on. They lived in Austin and begat our two cousins Sharon and Shelly. Dad formally John Estall Berry Jr. married Barbara Standish Walker. They begat two daughters Dana and Leah. By rights Dana should have been Barbara Standish Berry to carry on tradition all the way back to Barbara and Miles Standish but Dad felt the need to break tradition. Celebrating each birth from Ernestine and Dad Pop sent a twenty-five dollar savings bond. Seven years later Dad and Mom begat John Estall Berry III. Pop sent a check for one hundred dollars. The story was published in the "Loudoun Times Mirror". "One Grandson Worth Four Granddaughters." Since the check was written out to Johnny, Mom and Dad took it to the bank in Purcellville. The bank said it was fine and had Johnny put his footprint in ink on it as an endorsement. Mom still has that check.

Hugh Allen Walker or Gramps Married Barbara Standish Bense or Ramee. They begat three children. Mom's older brother Joel Malcom Walker Uncle Joel, Mom and her younger sister Deborah Gail Walker Aunt Debbie. Many years later my dear gearhead son-in-law Chris asked if we were related to Walker Mufflers. Why yes we said. "Then how come you aren't rich?" he asked. Not to delve into too much detail but, way back Gramps and Uncle Joel lost out due to some shady deals back then and gave up their parts in the business.

My sister was born at Cherry Point, N.C. Dad was in the Marines going on 8 years. He was planning to reenlist, but when Dana was about to be born he couldn't get out of practice maneuvers to be with Mom. He got out of the service after that since he felt he didn't want to work for a company that cared so little about family matters. He went back to Texas with Mom and Dana and got a teaching degree at Texas Tech. I was born in Lubbock.

Long about 1956 Gramps and Ramee purchased a 15 acres in western Loudoun County in Virginia. There was a seriously run down stone main house which used to be a girls school. They turned this old place into one of the finest houses still today in Loudoun. There was also a separate much smaller house the original house on the property built sometime in the 1700's which they turned into a guest house and a stone bank barn circa 1910.

Gramps got a tip or something on a deal on the ground floor of plastics. He invited Dad up here to also get in on it with the promise of a job. So when I was about nine months old Dad, Mom, Dana and I moved to Virginia with a bright future ahead. Shortly after moving the deal fell through. Gramps was a go-getter and did many things in life but he missed out a time or two. Gramps felt bad and gave Dad and Mom the barn, some start-up funds and five acres. He said, "Since you aren't doing anything right now turn that barn into a house." Knowing Dad hadn't really done that much construction we don't know if Gramps was trying to set him up to fail but that kind of thinking wasn't part of Dad's psyche. Dad surpassed everyone's expectations. He also got a teaching job in Loudoun and here we stayed. Ramee was ecstatic to have her daughter and grandkids close at hand.

Mom at barn before construction

Our first home the guest house. Ramee and Gramps raised baa lambs

Pop, John Estall Berry III and Penny

"Keystone" the main house and guest house.

NICHOLS HARDWARE

A ll those whatchamajiggers we sorted didn't just appear out of nowhere. They came from Nichols Hardware. Dad didn't mind taking Dana and I there when he needed some. We were well behaved enough. Old Mr. Nichols let us play in the big seed bins full of sunflower seeds and corn. We shoveled them up with the grain scoop and dumped them back in the bin listening as they fell in with a satisfying crackly sound. Kind of that same sound made as Rice Krispies made spilling into your morning breakfast bowl.

Dad not only got his whatchamajiggers there but also some of the best stuff ever. Most of the best stuff in the store was hanging from the ceiling. Dad noticed as we oohed and ogled over the contraptions hanging way out of reach. The color red must have attracted him because one Christmas our main presents were shiny red fire engine peddle cars. Later we also got our first bicycles there also red. I am pretty certain my first red and white tricycle came from there as well, but that is a story for later.

Dad was one of a select few people who could apply book knowledge into practical outcomes. Most people I think either read books, but couldn't seem to put that knowledge to work. Then there are those people who don't really read but learn their trade by watching others. Dad learned most of his exceptional woodworking and automotive skills from self-taught book learning. He was always tinkering at some project or another. He knew how to apply his skills and I think he just loved the tinkering process in general. One day however his tinkering did not turn out so well.

You see our red bicycles were becoming worn out so he decided to fix them. It ended up not as we expected because Dad decided to turn our two bikes into one tandem bike. I'm sure he figured out all the mechanisms and so forth and presented us with our newly improved version of mobility. Dana and I looked it over and knew exactly what we were supposed to do with it, but we could never summon the courage to try it out in fear for our lives.

Later that day Dad felt bad I guess and made us some stilts instead. Shortly thereafter we went to Nichols. Dana got a yellow banana bike. I got the bike of my dreams. It was a shiny purple three speed Schwin. For hours on end I did tricks on it up and down our smooth asphalt driveway. It was so balanced I could put my feet on the pedals, stand up and raise my hands and fly like the wind.

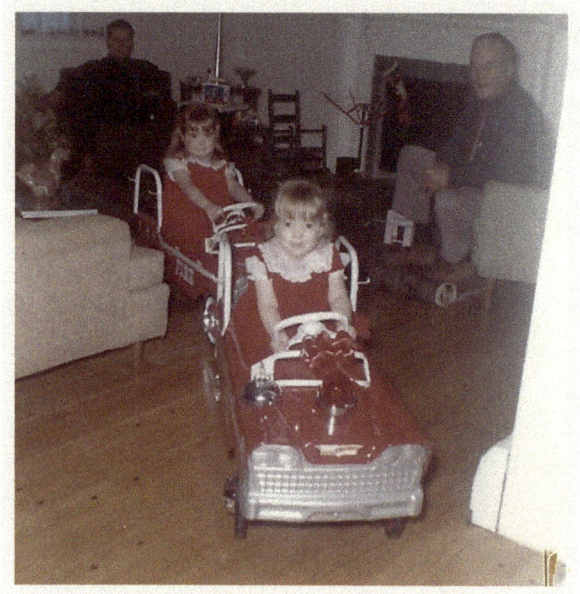

Red fire engines

Perfectly paved driveway

Gramps, Dana and Leah at the bay window.
Check out the icicles on the Christmas tree.

FRIENDS

My parents John and Barbara Berry were blessed to meet two of the most wonderful friends any young couple could have in John and Belle Ware. They were our other parents. Mom and Dad Berry lived at one end of Hillsboro and Mom and Dad Ware lived at the other. Belle mentioned once she and Mom met at Hill Tom Market but she wasn't sure if they would hit it off because when she first saw Mom she was dressed to the nines. Dad Ware was in electronics and also repaired TVs. Dad Berry was quite frugal minded. He had a lesser known Hallicrafter TV which were only made from 1950 to 1959. I'm not certain when our Dad's met but they got to really know each other because Dad Berry insisted the TV could be fixed, but Dad Ware was far from convinced. There were numerous discussions over that TV. Dad Ware finally determined the TV was beyond repair. They finally agreed to disagree but respected each other's opinion.

One thing I vividly remember is when Paige their younger daughter and I met. Dad and Dad were in our parking lot discussing something probably the TV for all I know. Paige was clinging to her Dad's leg. I was clinging fast to my Dad's leg. The two of us were peeking around but neither of us dared let go of the death grips we had on our Dads. Finally, not being able to concentrate on each other they peeled us off of themselves and said, "That's enough now, go play." We did. We played and played for years.

Belle and John had an older daughter Vicki the same age as Dana. They too became the best of friends. They had a younger son named J.W. A few years later both Mom Berry and Mom Ware had Johnny and Mark. J.W. was the odd man out. He became the tagalong. It wasn't all bad though because we frequently used him to our advantage.

When Mom and Dad met the Wares they lived in a tiny bungalow below Hill Tom Market. In 1965 shortly before Mark was born they bought a huge Victorian home on a property behind the bungalow. This house had sat vacant for quite a time and it needed serious attention to make it habitable. They saw its potential just as Dad did with the barn. It was Belle's fervent hope they could be in it by Christmas, so both Dads worked tirelessly and moved heaven and earth to make it happen.

In this life not many people are blessed with true friendship. True friends don't just come around when they need something. John and John built a friendship where you didn't keep score. It wasn't based on I'll help you do this if you help me do that. It was based on Hey, let's tackle this and then we'll tackle that. This may not seem such a big difference to some but trust me, the difference is epic. Slowly and surely both houses were renovated and improved. Surely and steadily John and John's friendship grew. Belle and Barbara's friendship flourished likewise. Belle and Barbara have been and still are the best of friends to this day.

John and John even always busy with so much still managed to design and build a BBQ pit for the Hillsboro Elementary School. They also became the self-appointed chefs of "their" BBQ pit. The PTA frequently hosted Chicken BBQ dinners. The ladies fixed the rest of the grub. We kids helped by taking the licked clean empty trays to the dishwasher always getting praise from our satisfied customers for having eaten the best BBQ chicken ever.

THE FOOD PANTRY

We had another wonderful room just off the kitchen called the food pantry, not to be confused with the butler's pantry. All of our usual staples were stored there. It kept flour, sugar coffee, Crisco and canned goods, dog food and paraffin wax. The wax served dual purposes, great for canning jelly and good for waxing sled runners. All neat and tidy on shelves Dad built all around the pantry mostly due to his love for a place for everything and everything in its place. The most special items placed in there and proudly displayed should anyone venture in once opening the double louvered doors were neatly stacked and sorted jelly jars. Of course we had grape jelly and strawberry jam but we also had cinnamon or crème de menthe pear, apple, mint, elderberry, cherry, blackberry, raspberry, peach preserves, cinnamon applesauce, tomato aspic and everyone's favorite homemade orange marmalade. What a kaleidoscope of color, a rainbow of delectability it was to witness. One can only imagine how many loaves of Mom's homemade bread were toasted back then.

Vicki, Dana, Paige and I had a whole other purpose for this utilitarian closet of sorts. We invented a game and we used tagalong J. W. to our advantage to play it. The other items we required for our game were the louvered doors which rattled if you banged on them and our little Toy Fox Terrier dog named Penny. We titled this game officially, *Let's Lock Penny in the Pantry and Make Her Chase Us*. We referred to this exact title every time we tried to get away with playing it.

The rules were simple. Step 1. Lock Penny in the closet. Step 2. Bang on the doors and make her nuts. Step 3. Elect someone to open the door. Usually the one with this part was at a disadvantage so since J.W. was handy we most times gave him this duty. Step 4. Beat feet and scramble up the back stairs to Mom and Dad's bedroom then through the nursery and across the landing and finally jump on Dana's bed which was tall enough Penny couldn't reach us. We had to haul J.W. up by the seat of the pants with barely inches to spare from him getting nipped at by Penny. We won! Hoots, hollers and shouts. Giggles and glee as we defeated our foe and Penny was barking and jumping but could not reach us safe on Dana's bed.

The only problem we suffered by playing our game was facing the consequences. Did I mention our house amplified sound? Thought so. So we are all up on the bed cheering our success while our parents were trying to enjoy a peaceful evening of conversation down in the living room. Our Dad parents came barreling up the stairs thundering, "You do not go trampling through the house like a herd of elephants. They made us all come down the circular stairs and sit on the first step in time out. If we picked at each other or pinched or even looked at each other the wrong way during this never ending punishment more time was added. We'd keep blaming J.W. the youngest on most of the added time. That poor boy couldn't catch a break.

PLAYTIME AT THE WARE'S

When we went to the Ware's whose house was nestled snugly up to the east side of the Short Hill mountain, playtime always meant we'd be completely worn out and ready for a good night's sleep. I believe John and Belle Ware took some hints from Mom and Dad after numerous attempts of *Let's Lock Penny in the Pantry and Make Her Chase Us.* Kids play outside! We came up with a new game or at least it was to us called, *Run Around the House Ball Tag.*

Simplest of rules ever or so we thought. *IT* has a ball. *IT* chases the others around the house and tries to hit them with the ball. If successful the person hit becomes *IT.* We faced only two drawbacks in the actual playing of this game. The first was deciding on who was going to be the first *IT.* This usually took more than one or two renditions of one potato, two potato, three potato four. We saw through that decider though quite keenly. If four people are playing you knew right off the bat who was going to end up five potato, six potato, seven potato or. It helped a little but not much when J.W. was old enough to add his extra fists into the countenance which sort of threw off the pattern. After giving up there was rock, paper, scissors and then "I was *IT* last time it's your turn!" Pretty soon Mom Ware came out and tired of the squabbling declared someone the first *IT.* The second issue we had involved the house itself. The backside of the house was fairly level but the side and front landscape sloped down a hill. If you missed your target you had to chase the ball practically all the way down to the field. *IT* now frustrated did everything possible not to miss the next target and finally succeeded hitting the next *IT* as hard as possible.

Unfortunately too, this game had no real winner. You just kept playing until you finally dropped to the dirt from exhaustion.

After a period of recovery we decided to tramp down to the springhouse. Dad Ware was always in there tinkering with TVs since part of this oasis was his workshop. As soon as you stepped in you felt an immediate relief from the hot sun. We heard water gurgling in the trough and took in the damp musty smells. We couldn't really stay long because the shop was small and we sensed we were in the way. Dad Ware's shop was crammed full of gizmos, gadgets and miscellaneous repair parts. We especially liked the glass screens and light bulbs. We were careful not to rummage around too much, but some odd items just screamed out to be more fully examined. We never knew what all it took to actually put a TV together. We thought if he had put his mind to it, he could have quite easily assembled a robot to rival or best Robot B-9 in *Lost in Space*. We even kidded around waving our arms about a time or two yelling, "Warning, warning." This did not put Dad Ware in a good mood. Still all those spare parts deserved some exploration. Had he actually decided to build a robot, I am sure he would have included spare parts from Dad's old Halliicrafter TV he got stuck with just to prove his point. Finally after all the hospitality he could muster, since Dana and I were guests, we were all told plain out to find somewhere else to be. So we did.

We went to the creek to catch crawdads. Never seemed to remember to bring a bucket so we'd just grab them, easier said than done. We studied them and let them try to pinch us and then plopped them back into the creek. We knew we had to be mindful of snakes, but one or more of the Ware's dogs were always nearby so we didn't worry too much. Once we determined we had pestered the crawdads enough or at least scared them all off, almost in unison we rallied our battle cry, "Let's go up to Mr. Wright's and see if he'll give us free candy."

There were two stores in town almost side by side Hill Tom Market and Hillsdale Market. The owner of Hill Tom was mean old Glenn Roberts. He hated kids because they stole from him. Dana and I knew that firsthand. Once we went in there with Dad. The Lifesavers and penny candy were right in front of us under the counter, and while Dad was paying we each lifted a piece of Dubble Bubble gum. Later on that day, Dad caught us chewing our contraband and asked where we got it. We had no choice but to fess up and Dad marched us right back to the store. We had to apologize to Mr. Roberts and promise never to do it again. We were miserable that day, but we faced the consequences.

Mr. Wright owned Hillsdale. The battered old sign said he used to even sell gas but when we went there wasn't much of anything to be had. Still Mr. Wright was there sitting next to his checkerboard and potbellied woodstove and invited us in. We were always very respectful to him. He asked what we were up to and he told us stories. We sat on his lap and gave him hugs. He was like having a spare grandfather. We loved visiting him. He seemed lonely. We didn't know why he was alone but we didn't dwell on it. Then he asked if we wanted some candy. "Yes please," and "Thank you." when he gave us each a butterscotch, Mary Jane or our favorite Tootsie Roll. Once he gave us all a huge Tootsie Roll but told us we needed to share. We didn't mind at all. We weren't about to eat our benefactor out of house and home. After a good visit we left promising to come back soon.

After a long day of sweaty, grubby play it was bath time. Mom Ware stripped us down and checked us for bumps, bruises, scrapes, scratches and especially ticks. We all slipped into the bathtub and Mom Ware added a goodly squirt of Mr. Bubble. We didn't start washing right away. We were too busy trying to get every last bubble we could out of that squirt. I suppose you know shampoo and regular soap counteracts the bubble making effect. We sure knew that but pretty soon Mom Ware came in and told us to start scrubbing. We went from filthy to frothy in short order. Time to turn on the spicket to rinse and then the unthinkable happened. No water came out of the spicket. We started shutting our eyes to avoid the dreaded soap in the eye. The only choice we had was to start yelling, "Dad help! Dad there is a frog stuck in the pipe!" Dad ran down to the springhouse and unstuck the poor creature from the pipe and a few minutes later the much needed rinse water started flowing again.

The Ware's house

The springhouse Dad Ware's shop

MORE ABOUT PENNY

We went to Spur, Texas to visit Gramma and Pop. Dana and I were still toddlers. While we were there Gramma had a friend and wanted to know if Dad could go and tune her piano. Dad never really learned to play, possibly out of rebellion, since Gramma taught and Ernestine played beautifully. He could tune pianos and supplemented his income doing so. In later years, he told me about his trick of the trade. He knew two songs by heart. Smoke Gets in Your Eyes and Sentimental Journey. When he was done tuning for a client, he played those songs with flair and embellishment. The then happy customer suitably impressed gladly handed over the money.

As a favor to Gramma, he went to tune her friend's piano. While he was tuning it, he began to smelling a horrible stench and he heard yapping. Gramma's friend said she raised and sold Toy Fox Terrier pups. Dad asked if he could see them so she took him to her basement where what poor Dad witnessed made him want to gag. He saw dogs in cages with toenails so long they were stuck to them. The filth and squalor was almost overwhelming, but Dad felt he needed to keep his composure at least for Gramma's sake. Today he'd have been first to call the law, but back then there was little he could do so instead he made the woman an offer. He asked if instead of charging a fee for the tuning could he possibly have a puppy for his daughters. The woman agreed and so Dad brought home a little puppy. He figured he couldn't save them all but at least this little one wouldn't suffer a cruel fate.

Dana and I were overjoyed. She was so tiny. We sat on the floor, spread our legs touching our feet together making her a little corral.

She was too small to even jump over our legs. At some point, somebody said "She's no bigger than a penny." Glances were exchanged and she had a name.

Another tidbit about Penny was best mouser ever. Dana and I had a huge bathroom to share. Dad made cabinets under two sinks. There wasn't much in them but towels, extra toilet paper and comet. Every so often we heard scuttling in this expanse, so we invented a new game called "*Let's lock Penny in the cabinet and make her chase the mouse*". Surely enough we'd grab her up, shove her in and shut the door, listen and wait. Clunkity, bumpity, scritchity, scratchity, yap, yap, yap, snarl, snarl and then at last all became quiet. We knew she had taken care of business and we let her out praising her for such a good job. Way better than our lazy cat Dum Dum. He hunted too, but usually outside chipmunks and birds. I wasn't fond of Dum Dum picking on them.

We later found out why Penny became such a good mouser. It seems Dad and Mom heard a mouse in the food pantry one night. They put her in the pantry to see what she would do. Penny cornered the mouse but intended to just play with it. Then the mouse turned on Penny and bit her on the nose. That was all it took. From then on Penny thought to herself, "Never again, that's it. Death to all mice." We also learned when we found out that story, we weren't the only ones who had locked Penny in the closet. How come we were the only ones who got in trouble for it? Dad? Mom? Hmmmmm....?

OFF TO WORK WE GO

When Dad taught school he sometimes took Dana and I with him on teacher workdays. He wanted to give Mom a break from us since she had little Johnny to tend and a huge house full of dishes, laundry, centipedes, spiders, crickets all named Jiminy and my favorite granddaddy longlegs to clean. I used to study on these long legged little guys. I couldn't figure how they could coordinate their legs without getting them tangled. I once watched one crawling across the living room carpet. All of a sudden one of his legs snagged the carpet. He struggled then he yanked and his leg ripped off. I was enthralled as I watched him keep going with now only seven legs. The most unsettling part was as he went on the leg he left behind kept twitching. Oh well, enough about that we were talking about going to work. We went to Leesburg and sat in the huge school desks in Dad's classroom and drew. Well, mostly Dana drew. There wasn't much to read so I squirmed around and got bored real quick. Dad sought the janitor and he let us go to the huge empty gym and got us a basketball to keep us occupied.

Later on, Dad worked in real estate so we went with him to House of Lords also in Leesburg. There we met a former basketball player named Fred Hetzell. The building was ancient. The back stairs were really steep. Fred was so tall he had to bend down to keep from hitting his head. Somebody put up a sign at the bottom of the stairs that said, "Watch out Fred." It was funny every time he almost got beaned. Dad didn't seem to mind taking us to work. He even used some of the time when he didn't have clients to try to teach us new math. He got all the books so we could get up to speed. Little did we know even he gave up and wanted to throw the books out and he had taught business math for Pete's sake. We didn't mind going with him because we knew we would more than likely get to have lunch from the Mighty Midget Kitchen. Best hamburgers on the planet. Just ask anybody. Many days at House of Lords and later at Heritage '76 a company he started we got to help Dad do crossword puzzles he loved to do when he was on duty. We spent many days there just being kids or pestering George Beere and John Devine two of his fellow realtors.

Dad was always eager to teach us stuff. He was glad when he could answer our queries. Every once in a while he probably regretted it. Getting to work was also fun we thought. Maybe to Dad not so much. Hard to enjoy the drive with two little chatty, giggly or bickering girls in the back seat. We couldn't play license plate alphabet game since there weren't enough cars to bother with and same was true with road sign alphabet. We memorized every sign between home and Leesburg. By the time we got to L we were in Leesburg anyway. My favorite sign to look for was the one signifying the little town called Paeonian Springs. I always wished Paeonian was spelled Paeonon. Then you could take off the Pae and the Sp from Springs and get a town called Onion Rings. I am sixty-four years young now and go by that town almost every day and it will always be Onion Rings to me.

One day we asked Dad what the yellow and white lines painted on the road meant. He told us. From then on he regretted having taught us because from that moment on Dana and I knew our mission was to help Dad drive. We scrambled to the back window and chanted, "We can pass. They can pass. Yea, everyone can pass! Aww, nobody can pass." We chanted this over and over, time after time and drive after drive. Pretty soon, Dad was kicking himself and clenching the steering wheel.

One day Dad tried to distract us from "helping" him. Passing by Godfrey's farm he implored us, "Look at the cows." We were nonplussed. We had five Black Angus cows at home not to mention also two donkeys named Lady Byrd and Jackie. We knew farm animals and I wasn't too keen on them anyway. Whenever you got up close to the cows they had flies buzzing around their noses and they had to lick at them to keep them from going up their nostrils. I thought the poor things looked miserable.

Another day on our familiar route, Dana and I were just getting ready to scramble to the back window as we were passing Grubstake farm. Wouldn't you know it these two silly cows were right by the fence trying to play leapfrog. They weren't doing a very good job at it either. The one in back trying to leap over the one in front had horns as I recall. They were both so big and clumsy and we thought if they can't even jump over each other, good luck seeing them try to jump over the moon. Then Dad heard our excited cries. "Look at the cows Dad, Look at the cows. What are they doing? Are they playing a game? Look Dad Look!" Dad didn't say anything, not one word. I didn't know it then, but I'm sure he was thinking to himself, "Oh great, what great timing for those two cows to be doing that right out in front of God and everybody." We finally gave up quizzing him and he must have felt a little relief when he soon started hearing, "We can pass. They can pass." from the back seat once again. He went home and told Mom about it that evening. He told her he just couldn't find words. One things for sure. He never asked us to look at the cows again.

The Mighty Midget Kitchen

THE CHINESE CHESTNUT TREE

Ramee an avid gardener, loved ornamental specimen trees. She convinced Dad to plant a Chinese Chestnut tree or Castenea Mollisima near the garage and kitchen door. It was not a tree any of us knew about, least of all Dad. Had he known more about the tree before he planted it he'd have flat out refused. Still in time I think that tree kind of impressed him. It had many hidden talents.

As the tree grew, we found out there was not one single season it was not doing something obnoxious. In the spring it spit out its flowers. These flowers had no business being referred to as flowers. They were long, skinny furry fronds. They were prolific. They also stank. As soon as Dad came out the back door coffee in hand, ready to greet the day he was greeted by a horrible stench. Your first breath might have well been your last. That tree just sat there saying, "Look at me, I'm right over here stinking up the place to high heaven." Dad thought it couldn't possibly smell like that all the time. He was right and much patience won out. Slowly much thanks to rain the "flower "scent abated somewhat.

The rain wasn't all good news. When Dad had the driveway paved he prudently installed a storm drain. As these fronds began dying and falling by the bucket load, they stopped up the storm drain and we had to scoop them out of it by hand. Raking them from everywhere else was no picnic either. But it was that or let them kill the grass.

In mid-Summer the tree started calling to us, "Now look at what I can do!" Those fronds were harbingers of spikey burs the size of golf balls. Those burs did house edible mahogany colored chestnuts. We didn't collect many of them. We preferred not to get stabbed to death trying to pry them out. Also Dana and I weren't much into wearing shoes. The whole time this tree was dropping its little land mines we only walked in a wide berth far around its perimeter, and even then if they took a good bounce a stray was lurking in the grass somewhere and you usually felt it before you saw it. Often we almost wanted to give up and put on shoes.

One family member who was not afraid of the tree was our cat Dum Dum. He climbed the tree every morning. Dad kept meaning to prune one of the lower limbs until he realized its purpose. Every morning Dum Dum perched himself on this limb which was about five feet off the ground. Aunt Debbie had a white German Shepherd named Sugar. Every morning Sugar came over from the main house to Dum Dum's perch to "get him." Every morning Dum Dum just barely out of reach hissed, clawed, scratched and peppered Sugar's nose until it bloodied. The blood was plain to see on Sugar's white fur. Once Sugar finally gave up he went back to the main house literally with his tail between his legs. The next morning he came back for another go at it. We asked Mom why he did that every day since he knew full well what was going to happen. Mom couldn't begin to figure that one out so we all just agreed Sugar was as dumb as dirt.

Dad enjoying morning coffee until he catches a whiff of the tree.

ANY NEWS?

CHAPTER 13

D ad installed a telephone in our kitchen. Prior to cordless phones Dad made sure the phone had a super long curly cord so Mom could still do dishes or fix dinner all the way across the kitchen. Soon though he got tired of seeing the unruly cord hanging all over the floor so in true Dad fashion he built a pine box to house it all. He frequently complained we kids were too lazy to stuff the cord back in the box. This box had a shelf on top for knickknacks and a side shelf for pens and a notepad. We affectionately called this elaborate piece of work the shrine. He even put a door on the box that housed the phone and cord so you wouldn't have to look at it just as a few people used to do with their TVs.

Dad's original intention for the shelf on top was supposed to be for knickknacks as I mentioned, but soon we acquired a kitten from the shelter. He was a relatively smart kitten but ended up with the name Dum Dum. Just for fun one day Dad put this kitten on the shelf. From then on it was Dum Dum's shelf. As years passed Dum Dum grew but the shelf did not. We started affectionately calling him Buddha Bulge Belly. He barely managed to stay on his shelf since most of his girth was wider than the shelf. His head legs and tail hung off each end and we prayed he wouldn't accidently roll over during a cat nap and fall off.

The phone was in part responsible for a solid source of income for one Miss Nettie Painter. On Friday nights we heard the phone ringing and knew exactly like clockwork who was calling. She wrote the Hillsboro column for the "Loudoun Times Mirror". She began her call in a spindly voice inquiring, "Any news with you folks?" She got paid a penny a word. If you didn't have any news to report you heard the miffed tone in her voice, "Nothing? Are you sure?" Fortunately more times than not, we were able to report Dana and Leah Berry spent the night at Vicki and Paige Ware's house, or Vicki and Paige Ware spent the night at Dana and Leah Berry's house. For weeks on end we were able to say we in part kept Miss Nettie out of the poor house.

Coincidently, Gramma in Texas also wrote a penny a word column for the Texas Spur called Library and Fine Arts. The biggest happenings in Spur where Dad was born happened at the Dixie Dog. If you didn't frequent the Dixie Dog you missed out on all the gossip. Gramma was getting discouraged and was about to give up writing the column, but then a new game came out called Trivial Pursuit. She carried the cards with her and supplemented her column with trivia questions. Bet Miss Nettie wished she had thought of that.

DUMPING THE DUST

I need to fill you in on our barn. Many people know Dad built our house out of a barn. I thought it was more like a castle minus the turrets and a moat. The walls and windowsills were 3 feet thick. The ceilings were very high and the hardwood floors were as sturdy as all get out. I remember when Dad installed the wood floor on the upper hallway to our bedrooms. We were allowed to help by pounding in the wooden pegs. What a racket we made. It wasn't just us making the noise. Our castle as most I guess must be are noise amplifiers. These acoustics did have a benefit, probably a godsend for Mom who was usually in the kitchen or laundry room. If we were happily playing or bickering she knew. She only needed to come when it was too quiet sensing we were up to mischief.

Most days Dad came from their bedroom down the hall to the nursery and then to our room to get us up. Dad was military and did not come in with a simple good morning. Instead he started bellowing as he approached, Turn to!" We did. Boy, did we! You got up then and there or faced the consequences. It's okay though really because every so often he would yell on a Saturday, "Turn to! It is time to dump the dust!" On those mornings you couldn't hop out of bed fast enough.

As part of the process of Dad building our castle he had a tool he used more than any other. He had a Dewalt radial arm saw. He built a work bench for it and included a trap door underneath. Once he positioned us under it he would lift the door and out came a bin full of sawdust right on top of us. This dust engulfed us with earthy pine and oak scents. We wriggled and squiggled around in our huge dust nest for a good while. Even getting dusted off with the broom was fun. Dad wasn't about to send two sawdusty girls back to the house and face the wrath of Mom. Having married a carpenter myself I often thought or spoke to him, "How I love the smell of sawdust in the morning."

Dana and Leah "helping"

Handcrafted dental molding using the Dewalt

BEING NAUGHTY DOESN'T PAY

T hank goodness for tetanus shots and penicillin. Every kid has heard the age old admonition don't run with the scissors! You'll poke your eye out! Dad's admonitions were much more specific possibly because they warned us against occurrences way more likely to happen. What were the chances of those scissors always ending up smack dab in your eye socket? Maybe not every single time, but all parents knew that's where they were headed.

I felt sorry for the kid it actually happened to and being a southpaw I was clumsy with scissors anyway. Ramee once gave me a catalog full of gadgets for left handers. Growing up I was spared being forced to become right handed. I never got any of the items in the catalog, but I thought it special somebody at least knew and most of all Ramee cared about how much we lefties had to cope in life. I wasn't berated for using the knife and fork backwards and scissors aside can openers were the worst but somehow I managed to survive.

So Dad had all this construction going on and he ordered us not to go near the huge concrete burn pit unless we wore shoes or we would step on a rusty nail. For some odd reason Dana and I were drawn to the burn pit like flies to our cow's nostrils. Plus right behind the burn pit were the two other bins and there we knew we could talk to Reverend Tracy and watch him turn the compost from one bin to the other. Short story Leah doesn't bother with shoes. Leah trots over to forbidden burn pit. Leah gets rusty nail impaled right into the arch of her left foot and has to go to Dr. Towe for a tetanus shot and worse has to suffer Dad not feeling sorry for her in the least because he ordered her not to do it.

While most of the rest of the house was transformed the attic was mostly left untouched. Vicki, Dana, Paige and I loved going up there to play. There was an old pulley with a bull rope we climbed and swung on. We knew better than to go near certain rotten boards up there which had suffered years of roof leaks prior to the restoration. We were also extremely careful to avoid the wasp nest near the north end of the building. Dad studied the attic carefully and deemed it safe enough for play except for one area. He plastered and insulated the stairs going up to the attic to keep heat in and to keep dust from filtering back into the house. The ceiling of the attic stairs was sloped and the upper side in the attic simply had plywood. He was afraid we'd climb it. Dad forbade any of us from climbing it. You could get splinters. Short story. Once Dad left the attic Vicki, Dana, Paige and Leah climbed the forbidden slope. Everyone slid back down. Leah slid back down and got a huge splinter in her butt. For three days Leah suffered in silence to avoid Dad's wrath. On the third day Leah said or did something naughty in the kitchen. Dad swatted her butt and she screamed like he had set her pants on fire. Leah fessed up and Mom and Dad closely examined the seriously infected wound. After attempting to get as much of the splinter out the rest was left for Dr. Towe. Dr. Towe determined Leah's tetanus shots were quite current and prescribed penicillin to counteract the infection. Dad didn't say I told you so. Dad didn't have to say it. I saw it in his expression.

Barn construction and the burn pit

Attic playroom

Scary end of the attic

PEANUT BUTTER AND HONEY SANDWICHES

Isn't it always the way with kids on weekdays? Getting them out of bed is a struggle, but on weekends we would get up and start making our way to our parents room. We knew we couldn't just come barging in. We knew they heard us coming as we heard them whisper the kids are up. We knocked and waited. Soon we heard, "You may come in now." Then came the barging in part as we were allowed to all pile up on the huge four poster bed. We had to help little Johnny make the climb. After good mornings and hugs we would say our line. "Let's talk about do today." That is exactly how we said it. Not grammatically correct I guess but it seemed to pull at Dad's heartstrings and always got the ball rolling so why mess with success?

Dad acted like he was taking time to ponder our request. Then he'd suggest this or that and we would discuss the merits of each plan suggested. Once an option was settled on he'd clap his hands and say, "It is official then, let's get to it." The one plan we always loved hearing as a suggestion was, let's go to the airport and watch the airplanes take off. We liked going to Dulles on occasion. We saw the wishing well, rode the escalators, my favorite part, and went up in the observation tower. But no even though Dad only said airport we knew he meant Washington D.C. and watching the planes was best done near Haines Point. This meant a whole day adventure.

Getting ready for our excursion took some doing. We needed provisions. Mom and Dad set about making a picnic lunch. We had lunch meat and Dad swore he knew the perfect way to construct a club in the proper order. Toast, Hellman's mayonnaise, lettuce, tomato, bacon, one slice of Kraft American cheese, toast, mayo, ham, turkey, second slice of cheese, mayo and toast then cut into four neat triangles held just so with frilly toothpicks. A sandwich made to impress Blondie's Dagwood. Still this was not to be on the menu today. We needed sustenance not elegance besides lunch meat might spoil in the picnic basket.

Dad began instead laying out slices of Mom's homemade bread. On one half of the slices he squeezed out honey out of honey bear. He was careful to make sure each piece was evenly covered. The other half got a good sized dollop of Peter Pan creamy peanut butter spread evenly as well. He didn't start slapping this delicacy together right away. He waited for the honey to start oozing into the crevices of the bread. As it sat it started making the bread slightly crunchy and stiff not runny. It's difficult to describe but worth trying. Once the honey had suitable time to absorb to Dad's satisfaction he then assembled and neatly wrapped the sandwiches in assembly line fashion. Doing even the simplest tasks made Dad happy when order and organization was involved.

Mom set about making a thermos of Kool-Aid. One time Dad thought to surprise us and brought home some Tang. We were excited to try it. How cool, the astronauts drink this in space! It tasted awful. We ended up having to drink it all because you didn't waste food but ugh. We were so glad once it was gone. It never came back in the house again. Dad said he felt very sorry for the poor astronauts.

All packed and ready, we set off on our adventure. We had front row seats as the planes did their very best to entertain us. From our vantage point we could practically wave at the lucky people lifting off. The engines were so loud we couldn't hear each other. We tasted the jet fuel and marveled at how the planes got in the air at all much less stayed there. Some of the planes whined, whistled and wheezed like the little engine that could believing in themselves to make it. "I think I can, I think I can." they thought to themselves. What a glorious time we had.

The way home was even a treat. Peanut butter and honey sandwiches can only make it so far. We stopped at Howard Johnsons for dinner. Before we got there Dana and I knew what was in store. Mom and Dad did not subscribe to the idea of children picking their own meals. We all had the fried clams, coleslaw and French fries. No matter how hard

Howard Johnsons tried those clams always chewed like rubber bands. Still we knew if we didn't give it our best effort we wouldn't get ice cream for dessert. We chewed and chewed and chewed some more until Dad finally took pity on us.

Dad in Korea. He loved those planes.

Dad on jet, love note to Mom

SALT'S OUT

G ramma sometimes called from Texas. She usually wrote us a letter and told us in it when she planned to call. At the appointed time we would assemble in the kitchen and wait for the phone to ring. Since speaker phones were pretty much unheard of back then we all huddled near the receiver to catch every word. Often Gramma was in the middle of a conversation and abruptly announced, "Salt's out." and hung up. Gramma had a three minute timer with an hourglass and as soon as the last grain of sand spilled to the bottom that was it. Her frugality sometimes annoyed Dad. He had to call her back and assure her we could continue talking since he was now paying for the rest of the long distance. We thought it was funny, somewhat quirky in fact, but that was Gramma. We could tell Dad missed his mom greatly especially right after hearing from her. He used to say how he wished he could take a big old lasso and rope up Texas and pull it closer to Virginia so we could visit more often.

Fast forward to 1978. Dana and I were in college. There was no such thing as paying your bills online. Dad received the telephone bill from the C&P telephone company. This particular bill had a listing of calls we made when we were home for the summer. There was no such thing as unlimited long distance. He checked each and every call made. Dad rechecked and scrutinized this bill and circled each call we made. He then sent us a letter along with the bill which I share verbatim.

Dana and Leah-

After becoming aware that you had abused the long distance privilege last month-- in addition to what was to be a lesson that money does not grow on trees—at least not on our tree—we hoped you would be more considerate! Obviously our conclusion is that the lesson was not learned or your brain is fogged or you just plain don't give a damn.

In the future any long distance call over three minutes or frequency of three minute calls, will become an automatic termination of long distance phone privileges. We would appreciate your portion of the bill by return mail.

Thanks-
Mom and Dad

Sure enough on the back of the bill he detailed each call we made. I'll admit I was the biggest offender but my then college boyfriend lived in Roanoke. I had made a whopping total of $26.67 worth of calls. Dana's portion was $16.72. Such unheard of amounts of money we squandered. Dad had every right to be angry. I have saved this letter all these many years along with so many others. This one stood out from all the rest of the just we miss you and love you letters. We all swear we won't turn into our parents and as Dad had to write that letter, I know without a doubt he was thinking about his mom's justified frugality.

Gramma's telephone timer

REVEREND TRACY

Reverend Tracy was Gramps and Ramee's gardener. I didn't know much else about him other than he lived south of Purcellville and had twelve children. He mowed, mulched, weeded, raked, pruned, tilled, planted seeds and was forever turning the compost. If that wasn't enough he was also my guardian angel. I can prove this fact without a shadow of a doubt.

One day I pedaled my little red and white tricycle to the front of the main house. I sat at the top of what we referred to as the pear shaped driveway. To this day I never figured out how this driveway got its name. It was a big oval asphalt driveway which began and ended at the main road. All I could guess was there was a pear tree in the middle of the oval surrounded by perfectly tended English Boxwood bushes. Maybe the tree was there first and the driveway was built around it. What I do remember was collecting so many pears from the tree for Mom's cinnamon pear jelly. Collecting them was quite a feat since by the time we got to the pears on the ground which were the only ones we could reach Dana and I had to dodge the swarming wasps, bees and ants also trying to get at them.

I sat thoughtfully at the top of this steep precipice looking down to the main road and surely little daredevil I could make it all the way down and stop before careening into the main road. What a thrill ride it was going to be. Visions of Evil Knievel and the like. I was five years old or so. I launched and immediately regretted it. Little tricycles have no brakes. The pedals were spinning so fast I couldn't get my feet on them so all I could do was careen off to the right where I met up with a three board fence and a rose bush. Within seconds Reverend Tracy appeared and detangled me from the tricycle, fence and rose bush. Ever so carefully he scooped me up and took me to Mom. He cradled me tenderly and knocked on the back door. As he handed me to Mom he said, "Little Missy hurt herself."

Playing in the back lawn of the main house was a trip to *Alice in Wonderland*. Irises, roses and other flowers too numerous to mention all gracing me arrayed in their splendor. Off to the side was Reverend Tracy tending to them. I watched him and studied his gardening tools. As busy as he was he patiently instructed me how to properly weed a dandelion. You have to dig as deep as you can to get the whole tap root or else it just keeps growing back. He let me try and praised me when I got out a really long root. I tried to do my best as I didn't want him to have to weed the same ones over and over again on my account. He had so much to do.

After my lesson I hopped and skipped around the yard for a while and thought to check out the ornate concrete birdbath. As I cupped my hands under the rim to stand on tippy toes to get a good look into it my fingers landed smack dab on a paper wasp nest. I ran hollering and screaming that little girl shrieking scream that tends to make adults skin crawl. Reverend Tracy came at once and after a quick assessment scooped me up tenderly and brought me home. He tapped on the back door and once again handed me to Mom with the familiar statement, "Little Missy hurt herself."

On another day I came home from kindergarten. I started to climb the circular stairs to my room. Sprawled across the first step was no less than a six foot black snake. I knew the drill. I didn't panic or make a fuss. Once relieved I avoided stepping on the poor creature, I regrouped and beat feet straight to Mom yelling, "Get Tracy!"

Ramee's garden and birdbath. More wasps!

LIZ

L iz was Ramee's live-in maid. She had her own private suite up some creaky stairs off the kitchen. A feisty, no nonsense little powerhouse always primly dressed in a grey maid's uniform with a lacy, white, starched collar and crisp white apron. She mopped, swept, vacuumed, dusted, made the beds, did laundry, polished the silver and prepared and served the meals. If that wasn't enough she also took it upon herself to watch Dana and I like a hawk. Ever up to mischief we would get caught and Liz would wag her finger at us and exclaim, "Now little missies don't you ever let me catch you doing that again!" What's worse we could be exploring any one of the many rooms in that huge house and always felt she just happened to be lurking nearby waiting to catch us.

When Dad and Mom were constructing the barn we lived in the guest house. Oh so many meals in the formal dining room in the main house. Dana and I loved breakfast the most. Dana especially since the closest thing to a vegetable she encountered was a potato. She probably picked out the onions if home fries were served. Ramee put the toaster on the table. She would ask us if we would like a piece of toast. "Yes please, Ramee." We minded our manners. We sat at the main table with the grown-ups mostly on phone books. Quite a balancing act but you quickly learned not to squirm around. Ramee would ask next, "Would you like your toast lighter or darker? "Lighter please, Ramee." was always the reply as it took less time. Ramee adjusted the dial to our preference and Liz stood at the ready with a bread and butter plate. Once the toast popped she laid the toast on the plate and Liz brought it around. "Thank you Liz." "Your welcome little missy." We were allowed to put our own Land O Lakes butter and homemade orange marmalade on our toast. We had to get enough marmalade on the teaspoon in one attempt. To dip again for another spoonful was rude and might chance contaminating the rest with crumbs.

Dinner proved a little more difficult. Usually it was edible except for liver night. Dana and I had to wait until the grown-ups were suitably engaged in political or current conversation. The dining room table extended to ten feet. Our inquisitive little fingers found and were attracted to a little shelf underneath. Dana and I used this convenient little shelf to hide that nasty old liver. Dana also stored her peas or lima beans there. Much better than to try to stuff them under her knife.

Did I mention Liz was an extremely thorough house cleaner? One day somehow she found our stash and wagged her finger at us letting us know not only what she found and knew we had done it and such. Ramee heard her chiding and scolding us from the kitchen. She came in only to witness Liz saying, "Now little missies I know what you did and it will never happen again." Ramee made us apologize to Liz. Consequences came left and right. Mom and Dad were told. Gramps was told and even Aunt Debbie. Aunt Debbie just snickered. Maybe she had considered if not had also done the same thing herself once or twice. Still punishment was duly meted out and we served our time. Even so, one thing we knew about Liz. She might have seemed like the tattle-tale but we also knew she wouldn't have bothered to correct us if she didn't care deeply about us.

There was a period of time I lived at the main house. Dana had a heart condition. Mom and Dad knew of this since she was six weeks old. It wasn't life threatening so the doctors advised waiting until she was older for surgery. When we lived in Lubbock where I was born, Dr. Arrington also advised Mom and Dad not to restrict her from playing. They took this message to heart. When she went to John Hopkins the doctors were pleased with her prognosis. They, as well as Mom, noticed she didn't act or look sickly. Other parents in the waiting room I was told, coddled their children treating them like invalids. Those poor kids looked in dire need. Even so, I can only imagine what Mom and Dad must have felt each day waiting until the doctors to do something.

As if that wasn't bad enough, Dana unexpectedly got nephrosis. This put a kink in the plans as her heart surgery had to be put off. Mom stayed in Baltimore with her in the hospital for six weeks. She stayed at the house of a loving family friend Anne Gonzalez to save hotel fees and so much driving.

I was too little to understand all this going on. All I could think was, "How come Dana gets to go everywhere and not me?" Dad was quite conflicted over excluding me but, all agreed and rightly so, I would be a distraction at the hospital. Ramee and Gramps gladly "sheltered" me in my family's time of need.

My first morning at the main house I awoke with the unsettling feeling of hey, where the heck am I? I peeked out from under the covers and looked around a bit. Oh, the wallpaper I recognized. When Ramee put me to bed the night before I had studied on the huge bouquets of roses and spider mums. I giggled when she said spider mums. What a silly thing to name a flower. They were comforting and I was glad they weren't real spiders I was so used to seeing in my bedroom in the barn. I looked around a bit more and spied the washstand with a porcelain pitcher and basin. Every inch of this now my room was fit for a princess. I'm the princess. This is my room.

I managed to scale down from the huge brass bed. As I lit I still felt a little out of place and desperately needed to find my Ramee. I crept across the landing to her master bedroom. Liz was hustling and bustling about. Then I spotted some old woman seated at Ramee's vanity. This old hag had long grey hair which cascaded all the way to the floor. I knew for certain it couldn't possibly be Rapunzel I'd seen in the fairy tale. I panicked. Terrified I screamed, "Where's my Ramee?" I ran from the room but shortly realized there was no place to run. I crumpled to the floor and let a temper fit engulf me.

As I lay there in this sorrowful condition Liz came out and scooped me up. She had to squeeze tight as I started kicking and flailing about to make her let me go. She was having none of it. She kept a firm grip on me and took me back into the room. She sat me down on the armchair next to the vanity. She wagged her finger at me and said, "Now little missy, that's enough of this. Now you sit right there and watch." I trusted Liz not to let anything bad happen to me so I stopped squirming and obeyed.

Liz went back to the old woman and started brushing and smoothing her hair. She rolled and twisted and pinned. She rolled her hair in sections and used quite a few hairpins and tortoise shell combs. I was still hiccupping a little but as she worked, it finally began to dawn on me she was bringing my Ramee back. I had never seen my Ramee before when she wasn't already dressed for the day. I went over to her and watched as she expertly applied her foundation, mascara and ruby red lipstick. After that she greeted me fondly and suggested French toast for breakfast.

Weeks went by and my time at the main house was pleasant. I couldn't shake the feeling Dad and Mom loved Dana more than me. Dana recovered from her bout with nephrosis. Now it was time to get ready for her heart surgery. Back to John Hopkins but this time I got to go along for once. On the way up we stopped at the Enchanted Forest in Ellicott City, Maryland. I guess they are trying to make it up to me I thought. I remember we all rode the Tea Cups and I peered into Peter, Peter Pumpkin Eater's pumpkin house. It was truly a magical place.

Once we got to the hospital Dana was admitted. We then had time to kill so Dad took me to see the brand new movie *The Sound of Music*. Gee, all these wonderful things Mom and Dad with just Dana and not me but I was dead wrong. Dana was envious of me when she heard I got to see the movie without her. Dad and I went back to the hospital and he explained this is where they had been taking her. It didn't take me long to realize this place was not some happy adventure for her. When we arrived Dana was in the ward with other kids. She saw me and started introducing me to some of her friends some of which she had remembered from her previous stay. One little girl had to live in an oxygen tent. Some had leukemia. One little girl stood out from all the rest. She seemed to be one of Dana's best friends. Her name escapes me. She was a burn victim and had one arm with no hand only a reddened, disfigured stump. Everyone called her Grandma Moses because she had been there for so long. I couldn't help but stare and felt sorry for her. She brushed it off and was sweet and friendly to me. The three of us cruised down to the nurse's station. I felt included. We met a great doctor named Doctor Lowe. All the kids loved him. He was as bald as could be. He always wore a long, white lab coat. He garnered the nickname Mr. Clean. After seeing all these new people and witnessing what the kids and parents were going through I began to realize just how selfish I had been when no one was paying attention to me.

SNICKERDOODLES OR MANGLING DAY

CHAPTER 20

(Either way, a treat in store)

We used to love hearing the telephone ring in the morning. One reason could have been because it was surely not Miss Nettie hounding us for news. It was usually Ramee calling instead. Ramee would ask to speak to Dana or me directly. "Good morning Ramee." At this point Ramee would announce her reason for the call. "Would you like to come over? Gramps is making Snickerdoodles." "Yes ma'am!" Hang up that phone and beat feet over to the main house.

From what we remember Gramps rarely spent time in the kitchen. He was almost always typing away in his den. Yet on this occasion he was in the kitchen and would feign surprise at seeing us at such an opportune moment. "Well, since you are here would you like to help me?" "Please may we?

Ever diligent Ramee made sure we washed our paddies first and fitted us with aprons and we set to work. Once Gramps got the cookie dough ready he brought it to us at the table. Cookie sheets were already laid out and he let us roll the dough into balls. He oversaw every detail of this task making certain our balls were evenly spaced and uniform in size. He never once hesitated to tell us to do better on the next ball or redo the one he thought inferior. Once he was satisfied with our ball rolling skill we were then allowed to roll the balls in cinnamon sugar and return them to the cookie sheet just so. Gramps popped the neat little army of dough balls in the oven and pretty soon the whole kitchen was filled with the most enticing aroma imaginable. Nothing on earth beats the taste of a warm Snickerdoodle still warm and chewy fresh from the oven. Gramps was Snickerdoodle chef par excellence.

Other mornings we received a direct call from Ramee. This time, "Would you like to come over? It is mangling day." Hang up that phone already and we raced to the main house as fast as our little legs could carry us. Ramee could always tell when we arrived as soon as she heard screen door slam. This time though we didn't head for the kitchen. We made a beeline for the basement otherwise known to us as the grotto. Just going to go to the grotto was half the fun. Once down the steep steps we knew we were going to encounter the best room in the whole house. Before checking it out though we peered into a smaller room off to the left. It had shelves with canned peaches and tomatoes and bins for potatoes, onions and sometimes carrots. The floor was dirt. There was a small window so it wasn't completely a root cellar but it was close enough to one. There was no door so we just peered in but never ventured in too far. The jars were quite dusty and looked like they had been there for years. Worse still were the spider webs everywhere. Anyone tasked to go in there for a jar of peaches for a cobbler risked taking his life in his hands. Probably a job for Reverend Tracy who wasn't afraid of anything. This room didn't need a door. The spiders kept you out.

We thought the best room in the whole house by far was the pump room. It was covered in stone from floor to ceiling. The floor was flagstone. The floor and walls stayed damp because there was a semi-circular pool also made of stone. It was built into the wall and water flowed into it from the mouth of a bronze fish. Since this fish was bronze he had a green patina and we thought him to be rather prehistoric. Still water splashed down from him and we thought it a good enough reason for us to also help with the splashing effect. We splashed our paddies in the water until we were nearly soaked to the skin. We splashed each other and the wall and each other until Ramee finally had enough and told us we had too. We knew better than to disobey so instead we turned our attention to the pump. This big black iron pump was taller than us. Gramps showed us once how it worked. It took all our effort just to lift and then pull down on the handle. Once primed we witnessed the water flowing when Gramps used it. Whenever we saw it we immediately thought of Helen Keller. We studied on it but knew better than to try it on our own. We considered turning back to the fish pool but remembered Ramee's scolding and also our real reason for being there in the first place. Knowing what was in store we left our little oasis and crept into a huge laundry room behind two heavy double doors. Liz quickly handed us a towel and we dried off a little. Then as we knew Ramee would, the first thing she said was, "Be careful now this is hot." At the same time we were also greeted by such an overpowering array of scents wafting about. The most immediate odor was Clorox bleach mixed with a scoop of 20 Mule Team Borax. I knew the Borax was in the box on the shelf above the mop sink. I never really understood what mules had to do with soap but I liked the picture of them anyway. We had that same box at our house and it just seemed as if it was as familiar as it was necessary. Once we just started becoming accustomed to these overpowering scents another one drifted toward us. We began to catch drifts of Niagara Spray Starch which Liz was dutifully spraying on the freshly scrubbed linens. This scent was also familiar to us being the one which greeted us when we opened the linen drawer in our dining room at home. We instinctively knew those prim and proper linens didn't just show up out of nowhere. They appeared due to mangling day. Liz then turned her attention to scrubbing the daylights out of the dirty linen infested with gravy stains, marmalade and occasional candle blobs which somehow escaped the bobeche.

Ramee was in full charge of the mangle. She was primly seated in front of a massive contraption which rolled and pressed the linens. The first time through they gave off steam since at that point the linens were still damp which always caused her consternation as it tended to fog up her glasses. Still she persevered. Some of the table cloths were up to 14 feet long. They were heavy and cumbersome but she dared not let so much as even one corner touch the floor. She kept up an even tempo using the foot pedal ever careful to avoid scorching. Each time they came off the roller she laided them neatly in front of her with great skill. As we watched this process we were mesmerized by how much dexterity this took.

We patiently watched and waited and waited some more. Finally once done with the big linens she allowed us in turn, to sit in her chair. She supervised us as we did the napkins. We had to be careful not to touch the hot press as we guided the rumpled napkins through and gently folded them when they came out flat as pancakes. We felt special Ramee trusted us and praised us for doing such a good job. We were glad we were helping.

Ramee's canned goods in the cellar.

WHOOPSBUMPS

Dad had a friend named Herbert Pearson. He was Dad's lawyer. He and his wife Shirley had two kids Carl and Ann. Mr. Pearson had a speedboat. He used to invite us to his river lot on the Potomac north of Shepherdstown, West Virginia. We loved going with them for picnics and waterskiing.

Dad drove our two toned Dodge family station wagon. Mr. Pearson rode shotgun. Mom and Mrs. Pearson comfortably rode in the back seat with my baby brother Johnny. All the rest of us kids were relegated to the cargo portion with the cooler, beach towels, spare flip flops and creek shoes.

Half the fun of the day was the trip. Once we hit Bakerton Road, a surprisingly well paved back road, we were in for a treat. Bakerton Road was chock full of whoopsbumps.

Kids are generally fidgety on road trips but not us. We didn't keep asking, "are we there yet?' Instead we craned our necks to see up ahead and knew when to start yelling, "Faster, faster!" Dad and Mr. Pearson gave each other a devious looking sideways glance as if to say, "Let's see how high they bounce this time." Dad revved the engine to the max and we took off. Every time we hit a whoopsbump, the car went airborne and so did we. Funny how when I used to ride the school bus, I used to ride in front clinging to my schoolbooks. Later on I grew to understand why so many kids scrambled to the back of the bus. They wanted to experience whoopsbumps on our bumpy country roads.

After being thoroughly rattled a dozen or more times, we craned our necks looking for the next marker on our journey. There was a railroad tunnel up ahead. Only one car could go through it at a time. You had to beep your horn before proceeding to alert oncoming traffic if any. Once we got to the tunnel, we covered our heads to keep a train if any from falling on us. Not certain why we knew to do this but it was part of the protocol on the trip and even better we knew we were much closer to our destination.

The first time we went I had a lesson in store. I was seven years old. The first time I saw the river, I raced down the bank to the dock. "The River " is what I remember yelling as I jumped off the dock. I had recently seen a 1953 movie called *Hondo*. In it Hondo Lane, played by John Wayne an Apache scout, threw 10 year old Johnny child actor Lee William Aaker who also appeared in *Rin Tin Tin* into the water to teach him how to swim. I suppose I didn't like the idea of someone else throwing me in. I was certainly capable of doing it myself if that was all it took to learn. Of course, up until that point, I had only been in water where I could touch the bottom. I wasn't well versed about the water depth or river currents. As soon as I went in I realized this was probably a bad mistake. I sank. I could see the sunlight above or below me; I couldn't exactly tell which. I tried to get to the light but didn't have the foggiest idea how. Also I had blown out all of my air mostly due to panic setting in. Thank God for Mr. Pearson my guardian angel, who saw me as I jumped in. He raced down the bank to the dock. I saw a huge hand. He must have seen my bubbles. Next thing I knew this huge bear paw snatched me out of the river like a salmon.

Once he got me back to the dock, he held me tight as I gasped, sputtered and puked my way back to breathing air. Then he fiercely lectured me about doing such a stupid and foolish stunt. I tried to come up with a reply, but I could only muster feelings of shame, embarrassment and gratefulness at the same time. Then he grabbed my hand like my life depended on it which it did. He took me back to the boat and shackled me into an orange life vest. He admonished, "I will never, I repeat never, let me see you anywhere near the river without this on!" "Yes sir" I answered meekly. Even though it repeatedly chafed at my neck from then on I obeyed without question.

As time passed, I have relived this event. I try not to dwell on my own whoopsbump but it tends To creep up on me at least once a year. When I watch *It's a Wonderful Life* when George saves Harry, I ponder what if............?

Picnic time was always yummy. Hot dogs, hamburgers, potato salad, potato chips and Koolaid to wash it down. Quite enough to keep us going but shortly after our meal we were stopped dead in our tracks. Our parents strictly adhered to and enforced the widely accepted, but later debunked myth of not swimming for at least 30 minutes after eating. I can't blame them for not wanting us to get paralyzing cramps. After all, the 1911 Boy Scout Handbook "assured youngsters a cramp would surely result from swimming before a meal had been fully digested."

Who knew? Parents that's who. Our parents in particular, we thought. So, since 30 minutes seemed an eternity, Carl, Ann, Dana and I invented a game to pass the time. We called it *Potato Chip Tag*. This is how we played it.

Put a bag of potato chips on the picnic table. We preferred Lay's BBQ chips but any bag will do. Assign a tree to be the safety zone. You had to physically touch the tree for it to be legal. Pick an *IT* by the acceptable method of one potato, two potato, three potato, four...... The object of the game is for *IT* to tag anyone who is not actively eating chips or not touching the safety tree. If *IT* questioned if you were currently munching, you could open your mouth to prove you hadn't yet swallowed them. If you ran out you could hightail it to the safety tree or try to make it to the picnic table for a refill. Unfortunately, *IT* soon learned to hover near the picnic table so it was wise to wait until *IT* ran to chase someone else before you could make a break for it back to the table of chips. The game usually ended if either 30 minutes expired or if the bag was empty.

Funny thing about that game. We were pretty much eating the whole time. Our parents rarely if ever made us start our time over. I guess they figured we had plenty of energy since we were running around like crazy and our food must have digested enough that we were capable of swimming and we probably needed to cool off anyway.

Waterskiing? We took turns. Your turn was over when you fell off your skis. I did okay except I wasn't thrilled about wearing the neck chafing vest. I tried to avoid the water whoopsbumps or wake of the boat. Never seemed to get the hang of going airborne in the water but I admired those kids who could.

Thanks once again Mr. Pearson for saving me from drowning that day. Otherwise, people wouldn't be reading "Dad Stories."

LITTLE ENTREPRENEURS

One spring Ramee and Gramps had a house fire. Dad and Gramps put together a crew to repair the damage. It must have been extensive because there were workers at the main house every day for most of the summer. So what do you do with two little girls who were most assuredly going to be in the way? Dad figured that problem out right quick. He built us a store. It started out with 2x4s and a shelf with compartments for our merchandise and after some cajoling Mom gave up a striped bedspread which Dad turned into a roof for some shade. He planted our store at a safe distance near the guest house where our customers could readily stop by. We were happy and safe and productive. Our store we thought resembled the Honey Store in the Bernstein book.

This wasn't just a typical lemonade stand. Dad had a knack for turning events into teaching moments. We had a cigar box for cash at first and he gave us some startup funds. I believe the initial outlay he funded was around two dollars. We had to pay that back. He took us down to Hill Tom Market so we could purchase supplies. We were scared to death to face Mr. Roberts but we had money to spend so with Dad's watchful eye we purchased penny candy, Dubble Bubble Gum match books and Kool-Aid. As our profits accrued we were soon able to expand our inventory and offered Juicy Fruit, Doublemint and candy cigarettes.

One of our most needed items we quickly learned to keep in stock was a can of Vienna Sausage. Every day a stonemason named Fred Lewis came and bought a can from us at lunchtime. Everyone called him Fred, but he hired a boy to help him. The boy once called him Fred and Fred said, "That is Mr. Lewis to you." We also respectfully called him Mr. Lewis. Without fail our little dog Penny would mooch off him. We watched everyday as he gave Penny the last piece of his last sausage. We also kept track of what items our customers preferred over others. Dana and I discussed the benefits of stocking more Mary Janes and butterscotch over peppermints and we learned to stock more of our better selling products.

It wasn't enough for Dad to just let us play store. He showed us how to keep a ledger. He schooled us at the kitchen table at night how to account for every penny. He taught us the proper way to count up from a dollar so we could make sure we were giving the proper change to our clientele. He even reorganized our cigar box and made us a better cash drawer so we could separate pennies, nickels, dimes and quarters like a real cash register. I am not so naïve to think we had many items unaccounted for such as gas it took for Dad to drive us to the store and ice and sugar and even paper cups to make and sell the Kool-Aid, but by the end of the summer we made a grand total of $32.16 profit. Dad gave us full rights to decide what to do with such a windfall.

Together Dana and I decided we really wanted a pool. Dad let us buy one of those corrugated metal ones with a plastic liner which then had to be leveled with sand underneath. I know now more expense and headache for Dad. It took forever to fill the pool from our well and probably only lasted for a month before it fell apart. Funny thing too about it was in order to keep us from drowning and near Mom so she could watch us it was right in the back yard in very close residence to the dreaded Chinese Chestnut tree. We learned many lessons that summer. The one which stuck in our craw the most was you get what you pay for. Looking back now the many lessons Dad taught us toward becoming self-sufficient adults were priceless.

Ready for customers

EASTER EGG HUNT

S hortly after the round elementary school was built, The PTA ladies thought it would be fun to host an Easter egg hunt. Community events brought people together and I am sure they were trying to drum up membership. Hillsboro Elementary didn't have that many kids and just about everyone attended with their parents. Kids are kids. Some relished the idea of collecting the eggs told there might be prizes. There were some kids who gave the hunting part less than a great whoop-de-doo. Some rather wanted to better spend their time on the see saw and monkey bars. Overall the hunt went smoothly until the end that is.

Dad had his opinions and wasn't afraid to state them. The ladies asked all the children to bring their baskets up to the long table. Dad noticed many in our baskets. He was proud of us and thought we did well perhaps we'd get a prize. Some finders in the group were just plain lazy he thought or they just didn't care. Humph, they don't stand a chance against my girls. Dad watched intently. The spirit of competition at its finest.

Soon he realized by watching the ladies they weren't counting the eggs. They began taking eggs out of the fuller baskets and dumping them into the baskets of the less fortunate finders. To say he far from expected this was an understatement. He marched right up to the table and confronted the ladies saying, "Just what the hell do you think you are doing?" The ladies quite taken aback said they didn't want any of the children to feel bad or left out. Dad couldn't believe what he was hearing. He yelled at these women, "You're teaching these kids they don't have to work for anything! Giving them handouts taken from the kids who did their best is wrong! This smacks of communism!" While the ladies jaws were still dropping he hauled us up and took us home all the while muttering how his kids are not going to be a party to such socialist practices. You keep what you earn. Don't expect handouts. Boy was he ticked!

EASTER EGG HUNT PART II

Mom and Dad Hawkins loved holidays. I'd have to say Easter was an eggceptional favorite. Every year it seemed the number of grandkids increased and so did the need for more and more eggs to be decorated for the annual hunt in their enormous backyard south of Purcellville. By the time 9 grandkids gathered we had up to 15 dozen or more to decorate. Each year we tried to keep up with new trends in decorating. Stickers, paint and most anything introduced by PAAS decorating kits were tried and the merits of their effectiveness were discussed at length. Mom Hawkins relished the job of being Decorator-in-Chief.

As years passed it also seemed Dad Hawkins had to keep up and revised his strategy as he was pronounced Egg Hider Eggstrordinaire. All the kids and grandkkids were ushered into the living room and admonished not to peek until Dad was done hopping about the yard. I know full well he was conflicted being tasked with this, but he could simply not get out of this chore even if he had wanted to. He loved doing this for the kids, but as I said he was under great stress as well. He developed a phobia which I think grew more desperate as each new year came. He learned he had to be the one to hide all the eggs because then he knew where they ALL were. And by ALL I mean every stinking last one of them! The reason I say this is due to the fact that one of those silly little eggs defiantly decided not to get found. That is until he found it when he ran over it with the lawn mower months later. For some reason his demeanor changed after that unfortunate incident. It seemed he started turning into an egg counting Nazi.

I first noticed this change one year when Lenny, Gil and Scott were cooking and cooling the eggs to be decorated. Every so often one or two split open while cooking and could not make it to the kitchen table. With saltshaker in hand, the cooks would gobble down the ones that didn't make it before they even made it to the egg salad bowl for later. I caught Dad once or twice glaring at the happy, egg gobbling bunch as if he wanted to them to knock it off or account for each and every one they inhaled which threw off the original count.

To make matters worse, one year brought about a newer and more confounding challenge. The introduction of the golden egg. It was later on accompanied by the silver egg specifically for the grandkids to find. Oh happy money. Glorious money. Evil money. Dad watched as his brood turned from being happy, giggling egg finding kids into lazy, greedy kids. Once someone shouted, "I found the golden egg!" Scott more often than not, or "I found the silver egg!" somehow it took the wind out of everyone's sails and the egg hunt would grind to a halt. Not acceptable in Dad's eyes. Totally eggsasperated he shouted to one and all, "You people get back out there and find every last one of them! The hunt isn't over until I say so.!!!!!!!" Happy Easter everybody.

P.S. My granddaughter is the eldest of her generation of great grands. She learned real quick. We took her to Lake Anna where Dad and Mom retired when she was about 4. We hid some regular and plastic eggs for just her to find. I was floored as I saw here running about collecting. What I didn't eggspect was for her to at such a young age pick up each egg she found. She put it to her ear. If it rattled she put it in her basket. If it didn't she dropped it back on the ground. Talk about a 4 generational curse. The cycle was complete.

A FAIRY TALE DEBAUCHERY

D ad was an exceptionally insightful person. When he noticed any ominous trend toward evil he didn't hesitate to let anyone within earshot know about it. He believed children should not be sheltered from the harsh realities of life. I remember him saying every child should be taught how to ring a chicken's neck. He emphasized by pinching his fingers together and swinging his wrist around in a swift circular motion to which he added a squackkking noise for effect. We were glad we didn't have chickens but we understood his point.

Of the seven biggest sins Dad's least favorite was probably slothfulness. At least it seemed to be the one he most railed against. Much in the same way the chicken exhibition was meant to teach us someone had to work at killing, plucking and preparing the chicken for it to be eaten, fairy tales he thought were meant to teach us good from evil.

Grimm's original fairy tales were meant to scare the hell out of little kids. Many other books I remember growing up also had the same effect. Ask anyone who remembers reading *Slovenly Peter* by Heinrich Hoffmann. That book gave us nightmares as intended but it taught us not to be like Peter or face ridicule. When grunge came into fashion where teens chose not to bathe or comb their hair I thought I'll bet those kids never read Slovenly Peter.

One of Dad's pet peeves was the fairy tale about *The Three Little Pigs*. In the original version the first little pig was lazy and built his house out of straw. Obviously no match for the wolf who hardly had to puff at all before devouring the pig. The second pig built his house out of sticks. This time the wolf probably had to use a little more huffing technique, but this pig also suffered a horrible fate. Dad was pretty fond of the third and more industrious pig who built his house out of brick. No amount of huffing or puffing budged the house even an inch and he survived the wolf's onslaught. Then some do-gooder came up with a less tragic story to supposedly spare kids from all this killing. Pig one and two ran to pig three's house. Oh goody nobody died. Moral of this newer version, go ahead and be lazy. Big brother will take care of you. Dad always felt sorry for pig three who from then on had to take care of two slothful, goldbricking freeloaders who refused to carry their own weight.

HANDMADE CHRISTMAS

Dana and I were used to going out to the garage to help Dad or just pester him in general. Imagine our dismay one year in November when all of a sudden the garage was deemed off limits. Not only locked, Dad put colored paper on the door and window panes to completely obstruct our peeking efforts. Why couldn't we go in? What had we done wrong? We didn't know then Ramee had given Dad an item which needed serious attention. Along with that Dad determined all our Christmas gifts were going to be handmade. Time passed slowly but Christmas finally came.

There were rules concerning gift opening. Stockings were first then a proper breakfast and later opening of the main presents. We were delighted to open our little wooden tic-tac-toe boards with colored wooden pegs. We also hoped to enjoy what Dad referred to as silly cycles. These contraptions were constructed with three wooden disks and dowels. Ramee had painted the disks with brightly colored spiral shapes. You put your feet on the dowels which served as pedals and off you go. They didn't work. We laughed and considered it a good try and tried to shake off the thoughts of the tamdem bike.

Our main present was too big to wrap. Dad covered it with Mom's bedspread and we were told absolutely no peeking until after breakfast. We were getting pretty tired of all this no peeking business but we minded. Still we couldn't help but speculate. There was a taller part and shorter part which with the bedspread on it seemed to resemble the shape of a car. We whispered, "It's a car. It has to be a car." Probably not motorized, but we thought it could at least be a peddle car like our fire engines were. We even started conjuring up thoughts about how the Flintstone mobile worked.

Breakfast done and tidied up Dad unveiled our main gift. The item Ramee gave Dad was a dollhouse. It was made for her by her great grandfather and was named Barbara Villa. It passed down to Mom and then to Aunt Debbie and now to us. When Dad first saw it he knew it needed some work. In true Dad fashion he wasn't about to be satisfied by fixing up the original. He built a big storage base for it and added an addition which became the kitchen and an upper patio deck. Not only that, he put in electricity. All the rooms had ceiling lights and the dining room had a chandelier made from one of Mom's rhinestone necklaces. What a stupendous work of art. We have an article from the "Loudoun Times Mirror" with Dana and I looking at it with the headline Dollhouse Passes to Fourth Generation. We liked it okay but we were rather disappointed it wasn't a car.

Dollhouse in the "Loudoun Times Mirror"

ROAD TRIPS

When Dad was teaching he had summer off. He and Mom decided to get a piggyback camper. They looked at many different models. There were many choices and I guess Dad was looking for a sign from above on which one to choose. One presented itself as plain as day. The one he chose had a dinette table with a map of the United States on it. He couldn't believe when he studied the map it actually listed Spur, Texas on it. Spur, Texas the town he was born was as unassuming as they come. The most frequented establishment there was the Dixie Dog otherwise known as the local gossip parlor. That dinette table said pick me pick me. Choice made.

That summer we toured most of the country. Dad totally refused to go to California and all we knew about it was Disneyland so we were a little disappointed but we survived. We saw Six Flags over Texas which was plenty of fun and enough to keep us from being sad over not meeting Mickey Mouse. We saw the Grand Canyon, Yellowstone, Crater Lake and Mount Rushmore to name a few of the more memorable sites. All in all it was a long trip but worth every mile. Speaking of miles it's a long time to travel between sites and we were really fortunate to have an eight track tape player or so we thought. Dad even let us listen to the Monkees and the Mamas and the Papas. Soon though he'd yank out our tapes and we'd start griping and had to succumb to listening to Ray Coniff and then Herb Alpert and the Tijuana Brass. Back then we didn't care to listen to each other's musical stylings but as I grew older I could fondly remember his choices. Later after that trip Mom and

Dad got another RV instead of a piggyback. They said the piggyback seemed top heavy.

We went to Maine in the RV. Dad didn't care to go to any tourist traps so we went way out along the coast. It was way better. We also went on a 4 day trip to Vance's Cove with the Wares. This plan was well concocted except it called for parents in the camper and kids in the tent. All well and good we thought except it decided to rain the entire time we were there. Five kids stuck in a soggy wet tent. We couldn't go out and we couldn't even play cards since they also were hopelessly wet. We tried bouncing a ball around for a while in the tent but soon realized we had only succeeded in compromising what little was left of the Scotchguard waterproofing on the tent. Finally enough was enough and we gave up and tried to come home. We tried to cross a creek to get out of there. Vicki, Paige, Dana, J.W. and I were all laying in the top bunk over the cab looking out the front window. The creek bed we attempted to cross had swollen substantially from the deluge. All of a sudden the camper lurched and lunged and we rolled back and forth into each other. We all thought we were goners, but miraculously Dad maneuvered this rolling death trap and we made it to the other side alive and well.

The only other trip of note I remember was going to see the Natural Bridge in Virginia and Ruby Falls and Lookout Mountain in Tennessee. We circled back through Hungry Mother State Park in West Virginia. Most of this trip we witnessed from the upper bunk. A trip through the mountains is nothing to sneeze at with such steep hills, deep grades and hairpin turns. I must say you wouldn't need hairpins after a trip like that since by then all of your hair would have fallen out from fright. Still, Dad maneuvered the whole trip and brought us home safely except for one thing. Fifteen miles from home we attempted to cross the trestle bridge on Route 9 east of Charles Town, West Virginia. Mom, Dana and Johnny were napping and so I was riding shotgun. The bridge was narrow and old. We met a truck coming from the other direction. Dad swerved just a little and in doing so smacked the rear view mirror clean off on my side right into the bridge. It scared the liver out of me. So many years later when Gil and I started looking for an affordable place to live in West Virginia, I was all for it but, I told him steadfastly in no uncertain terms would I even consider living on the west side of that bridge.

Dana and Leah at Mount Rushmore

SLEDDING

Having grown up in Texas where snow was not unheard of but much less frequent, Dad took it on up here in Virginia as he did with every challenge. He took on the blizzard challenge of 1966 in full steam ahead mode. Since we lived in a big, old, drafty barn there were many issues to address. When the blizzard hit and the power went out he had to contend with the possibility of frozen pipes and bringing in enough firewood to keep his brood safe and warm. He had prepared ahead and we were fine.

We kids meanwhile were happy to get to sleep by the fire in the living room in sleeping bags and not have to go to school. My brother didn't have to worry about anything since he was only about 8 months old at the time. Soon enough the not going to school for weeks part got old and Dana and I started feeling imprisoned. At least one thing we didn't worry at all about was having to go to the store for anything. Our well stocked pantry saw to that even including sterno to heat our meals.

I recently had to pick Mom's brain for more details about this whole ordeal. I was unaware at the time Dad and Mom had to trudge over to the main house to draw water from the hand pump in Ramee and Gramp's basement to do laundry and wash dishes and so on. I did ask her too, if she remembered if we lost phone service. She said we didn't. "Whew," I thought. It would have been such a shame if Nettie Painter had lost access to her penny a word income. It seems she was spared. I snicker a little when nowadays, people freak out over losing their internet access and such. "Nuff about that. We had real issues to address.

Dad could see we were beginning to get a little stir crazy. In my heart of hearts I could tell he was becoming the stir craziest of us all. Since he was teaching then he didn't have to worry about going to work. So instead he worked hard making sure we were going to have some fun.

The snow was so deep you couldn't see the cars only their antennas stuck out. There was no sense wasting time to dig them out right away either since the roads weren't plowed. We had a huge swale in our front yard and it created a snow drift beyond belief so Dad put it to his advantage. With some digging he created a snow fort, more like a snow cave. It had a front door and a window and he carved out a shelf on the inside. We put a candle on that shelf so the cave wasn't so dark and scary when we played in it.

Even though the cars were socked in he made sure his trusty, "red" Farmall tractor was not. If while reading the next part of this story I hope you are not one to tend to get squeamish. In today's world if anybody had seen what Dad did next, he'd have probably been thrown in the hoosegow for reckless child endangerment. As I am writing this now I can assure you we all survived and lived to tell the tale.

Dad gassed up the tractor and to it he tied with ropes and chains every sled we had. He did not forget to grab as much paraffin from the pantry as he felt was needed and waxed all the sled runners. He had concocted a plan with Dad Ware his co-conspirator. We hopped on the sleds and off we went. He drug us all the way through town and was mindful enough to speed up enough when we crested the big hill in the middle of town so he could surely stay ahead of us. We made it to the Ware's house and got ready for our sporting event. Both Dads got everybody hooked up and we made the grueling ascent up Stony Point road to the top of Thompson's hill. Anyone who is familiar with this stretch of road knows the hill descends back into town and is as steep as any bobsled course at the Olympics. Once at the top we unhooked our sleds. We sledded all the way back down into town. Even though it was technically a paved road we weren't worried in the least about facing oncoming traffic since other than the tractor there wasn't any. Once we reached the bottom Dad hooked us back on and up we went again. Once the Dads decided we were exhausted and cold enough we all met back at the Ware's house to warm up by their fire. I try not to banter this word about as it is sometimes overused but it fits in this case to describe the event. It was Awesome.

"Hey Dad, we found the car"

Dad's red Farmall good for mowing, great for towing sleds.

CARS

Dad loved cars. Truly he loved just about any contraption involving speed and horsepower. Let's just say he probably mostly leaned affectionately toward cars. The first car I remember was his Avanti made by Studebaker which at the time competed with Chevrolet's Corvette. We drove in it to and from Texas when we went to visit Gramma and Pop. Dana and I slept on the floorboard and Little Penny rode home in the glovebox. One day Mom, Dana and I were in an accident on Rt. 9. It wasn't serious thank goodness. There was damage to the right front fender and headlight. Dad fixed and repainted it in the garage. I remember we were all standing there admiring his handiwork. He told us not to touch it. For some reason I couldn't help it but no sooner than he said it I felt I just had to reach out and pat the car and tell him he was going to be okay. I'll go ahead and blame *Winnie the Pooh* on that poor choice. I had numerous stuffed animals and I believed they all had feelings. When I went to bed at night I tucked all my animals in with me. It took some doing as I put them in order biggest to littlest in layers and checked to make sure they all could breathe. I thought the hurt car had feelings so I tried to console it. I just wanted him to feel better. Needless to say I suffered immediate consequences. Dad swatted my hand and then my butt and told me to leave the garage NOW! I fled in tears.

Dad later turned that garage into a rec room. Gramps and Dad built a 3 car garage complete with a grease pit and a gas tank. Dad set up his workshop there in one bay. Sadly for Dad Gramps bought a Chrysler Imperial and housed it in the middle bay. It had huge fins and

Dana and I thought it was the Batmobile. We didn't like riding in it much because it had power windows. Those weren't the problem. The problem was Ramee riding in the front seat. All the way to church and back she kept telling us not to touch the buttons, or else. Dad's only pet peeve was it took up too much real estate in the garage and he had to be constantly mindful not to ding it.

Once Dad was in real estate he needed a fancy car to take clients in to show them houses. A series of diesel Mercedes soon followed and later on a gas powered 450 SE Mercedes which scared me as it was the car in which I took my driver's test. The trooper even tried to confuse me and told me to go the wrong way down a one-way street in Leesburg but I didn't. Hallelujah. I passed. I guess if the trooper figured my Dad felt comfortable letting me drive it, he wasn't going to quibble over passing me.

One of the neatest no, I take that back the neatest car Dad ever got was a 1950's Mercedes touring limousine. He had planned just to test drive it at Star Pontiac in Leesburg, Virginia. While test driving it he accidently dinged it and felt so embarrassed he bought it. It was gray and had gray crushed velvet interior. It looked like a German gestapo car. What he liked best about it was the window which rolled up and down between the front and back seat. He said he liked rolling it up so he didn't have to listen to us. We affectionately called that car "The Bomb". It sure as heck was.

I already told you Dad liked red but, when Dana got licensed and started getting summer jobs he bought us a fluorescent orange Comet. He said he wanted people to see us coming. One day he asked me to go down to Hill Tom Market to get gas. "Sure thing Dad." I pulled up to the pump trying my best to align the car. I heard a clompity sound. I got out and went around only to realize I had just run over mean old nasty Mr. Robert's gas hose. Luckily there was no damage but Mr. Robert's scowled at me something fierce. I apologized my butt off and was still shaking with fright by the time I got home.

MONOPOLY

D ad and I had a special bond. We were both highly competitive. After dinner sometimes we would get out the Monopoly game and Mom, Dana and Johnny scattered. As long as it wasn't a school night we could play six or 7 games a night into the wee hours of the morning. Impossible you say? We'd just divvy up the properties and start from the luck of the draw. If it was clearly obvious one person got too many monopolies from the deal we just declared a winner and dealt again.

Dad also taught me how to debate. We'd pick a topic and state our opinions. No subject was off limits. Dad admonished me to make certain I qualified my statements. At times we shouted or I broke down in tears when I couldn't convince him of my position. At this point Mom showed up and told Dad he was being too hard on me. She always tried to be the peacekeeper. Still sniveling, I'd tell Mom it was okay and back at it we went.

I loved school. I took every course I could except for math. When I was a senior at Loudoun Valley they started running out of elective courses and implored two of my favorite history teachers to teach Sociology and Economics. I took both. Mr. Blakeney taught Sociology. Trying to be innovative he arranged to take us on a field trip. Hastily planned and approved our class ventured forth. It didn't end so well for Mr. Blakeney. He wasn't fired but when parents found out where he took us thanks to a glowing article in the Loudoun Times Mirror they caused quite a ruckus. We had gone to St. Elizabeth's Mental Hospital in Washington, D.C.

On the first day of Economics Mr. Gillespie who had barely had time to familiarize himself with the curriculum started by telling us to turn to Chapter Three. Now in all my years of being a straight A, nerdy, bookworm and goody two shoes something spoke to me this just didn't seem right. I spoke out. "Why can't we start with Chapter One?" "Don't worry about it turn to Chapter Three." "No we should start at the beginning." Back and forth we went. By this time he was getting red in the face and announced, "Miss Berry if you are so sure we should start with Chapter One you will teach it! I expect you to come in tomorrow with a 30 minute lesson which I will judge and if it is not satisfactory you will sit quietly for the rest of the semester and receive an F!" That was my turn to become red faced from total embarrassment and humiliation.

I went home and confessed my plight to my Dad. He didn't chide or scold me for being rude to the teacher. He simply said, "Well let's get started then." Dad taught school, specifically Business Math and Economics. The next day I was fully versed and ready to teach the lesson called "The Island Economy" visual aids and all. I confidently related this lesson to my teacher and fellow students. I captivated them with my well planned and executed and at times humorous lecture so as not to lose my audience. My classmates, teacher and I learned from Dad if people live on an island they need a currency that is trustworthy so there will be peaceful commerce and not anarchy. If say your currency of choice is pukka shells your government tells you there are plenty of pukka shells sealed in the cave. A Fort Knox if you will, I referenced and could see the students paying attention. All trade and commerce continues. If say someone starts a rumor true or not, this Fort Knox is empty chaos ensues. In the seventies we weren't so far removed from stories of runs on the bank, Wall Street crashes and depression. This was also a topic of concern to everyone since we had gas rationing at the time. You could only get gas on even or odd days depending on the numbers on your license plate. Again my "students were paying strict attention.

I received applause and an automatic A+. Mr. Gillespie affirmed, "Well Miss Berry that was an excellent presentation. What do you suggest we do next?" Without hesitation, I proffered a Monopoly tournament. My team won. Better than that, Mr. Gillespie was interviewed and featured in an article in the "Loudoun Times Mirror" when he won innovative teacher of the year award. Thanks Dad.

THE POOL

T he camper sat for a while after our last trip. Mom and Dad began thinking it was becoming too expensive to maintain for as little as we intended to use it. Dad realized we needed a family meeting. We all got a vote. Democracy at work. The problem with this family meeting shtick was every time Dad announced family meetings he would begin with the statement, "I get 2 votes, Mom gets 1 and you three get ½ of a vote." Bummer. This time we hoped it was going to be different and there would at least be a consensus. The item up for discussion was the fate of the camper. Dad asked, "Should we keep the camper or sell it and buy a pool?" For a tiny moment Dana and I thought back to our first experience with a pool and shuddered. Pretty soon though, Dad had us breathing a collective sigh of relief as he laid out his plan.

This pool he envisioned would be a state of the art Anthony heated in ground pool with a decorative blue mosaic tile border. This behemoth was planned to hold at least 30,000 gallons. It had a welcoming shallow end with gracefully wide entering steps, a deep end, diving board and underwater lights. There was also a large surrounding cement patio. It was not planned to be plain old rectangular in shape. It was freeform and had a seat in the deep end. After studying the glossy photos of this proposed paradise on earth to put it mildly we never got around to voting. We just cheered instead and the meeting was adjourned.

Backhoe and bobcats, excavators everywhere. The diggers soon realized the deep end was going to be deeper than planned since they encountered a large portion of unexpected soft dirt. Rebar and sprayed gunnite, concrete, plaster, coping, tile, finishing layer of white plaster.

We were told this finishing had seashells or something in it and should last a lifetime. Plumbing, electricity, filters and heater to install. What a process to witness. We were starting to be glad the pool would be heated because we didn't think it would be ever finished before Christmas. Finally, the work was done. Now it was time to fill 'er up.

Unlike the Wares we had a well. The chances of a frog stopping up the waterworks was slim or none. Our well was shared meaning it also fed the main house as well as our barn. Dad was trying not to stress the well too much, but soon realized it would take a month of Sundays to fill. The contractors had cautioned Dad about waiting a while to fill it since the finishing layer needed time to cure properly.

Dad thoughtfully considered their words for probably a full five minutes or maybe a little longer but not much. Patience being a virtue didn't seem to be part of Dad's otherwise virtuous attributes. He was more of a let's get it done so we can get to the fun kind of guy. He went to Lovettsville and enlisted the help of the fire department to help fill the pool. They readily agreed to help. Sadly the fire department fellows were not privy to the admonition the contractors gave Dad. They did fill the pool. What we didn't realize until it was too late was they used water sucked from the pond on our old piano teacher Miss James property to fill the pool. I guess Dad just assumed they were going to use town water. Boy was he mad. Even after all the shocking, chlorinating and filtering that gorgeous pool had a brown stain in the deep end where the plaster hadn't quite cured.

The pool under construction

Way more fun than camping.

THE TINY STEINY

When Dana and I were in the fourth and fifth grade Dad wanted us to learn culture and refinement. He purchased a small upright piano. On Wednesdays after school we walked down to Miss James house to take piano lessons. At first we didn't mind the walk so much, but pretty soon it got longer and longer especially up the really long driveway. We went and learned and practiced at home when forced. Some of the things we learned was that sweet little Miss James always smelled of old, soggy, stale saltines. Another learning experience involved Miss James mashing our fingers on the keys or stretching them out on the keyboard we thought to the breaking point. Piano lessons did not continue on to the next school year.

The little upright sat in its place the living room untouched except for an occasional dusting. One horrible day in its life I'll never forget. I was bored and minding little Johnny. I spied the piano and climbed on the bench and put Johnny next to me and we started banging around a bit and I even tried to remember one of the few tunes I learned by heart. We were actually having a pretty good time, but then without warning Johnny fell off the bench and hit his head on the piano leg. That boy knew how to gush blood. He gushed and gushed, I screamed and Mom came running. A trip to Doctor Towe and stitches later we didn't try that again. I knew it wasn't the piano's fault but I could never look at it the same way again.

One day a few years later the little piano got its break into the big time. Dad was in real estate and had a love for entertaining. Aunt Ernestine, Gramma and Shelly came for a visit from Texas. We had a beautiful patio and an in ground pool surrounded by stately Weeping Willow trees. Dad invited friends, clients, colleagues and contacts to a piano concert. Everyone who knew Dad knew him to be quite a practical joker, but they also knew booze would be served so there was quite a turn out.

Dad took the little piano to the patio and transformed it. He tuned it and took huge cardboard boxes and two by fours and constructed a grand piano shape affixed to its back. He painted this grand shape black and after convincing Mom it was sturdy enough she let Dad borrow a silver candelabra from the dining room to place on it. We set up chairs and all was ready except for one small detail. Dad and I took a piece of yellow construction paper and in my very best cursive I wrote "Tiny Steiny" on it and elaborated the edges with curls and swirls for a border. We glued the name tag to the front of the piano above the keyboard. We hoped the little piano would feel proud of its new moniker.

Once people started arriving they were somewhat chagrined to see an actual piano by the pool. Dad wasn't kidding this time. Drinks were served and the candles were lit. It was dark and you could almost envision a real grand piano. The Weeping Willow caught the lights from the moving water in the pool. Everyone sat and Aunt Ernestine was introduced. She delighted all of us with exquisitely played classical and show tune music as she had quite an extensive repertoire. All was accentuated by the moonlight, stars, pool lights and candlelight. If you tried you couldn't have wished for a more magical evening.

TIPS FOR DATING MY DAUGHTERS

D ad was an exceptionally good host and loved a good party. I know I've mentioned this a time or two in Tiny Steiny but it bears repeating. He had secret or I suppose you could say ulterior motives when he threw the piano concert shindig by inviting clients, contacts and colleagues. It certainly increased his notoriety. "Hey, remember when we went to that great party at the Berry's House? Yeah, he's really a great guy. I'm going to get him to list our house." I know Dad thought these things through. Remembering back, cell phones didn't really come about until 1984. This was the 1970"s. He was quite the salesman.

"So, I now have two gorgeous daughters under my roof with raging hormones. How am I going to manage this?" he thought to himself. Dana was quite athletic. She played basketball and softball and more importantly she was a member of the Keyettes, the ladies league supporting all the jocks back in the day. These Keyettes had their hearts set on quarterbacks, defensive linemen, heavyweight wrestlers and basketball greats. So too, these high school stars had their hearts set on cheerleaders and so on. That is not to say Dana was just a jockette. She was on the honor roll to boot. The best part was many of all the jocks then knew their fifteen minutes of fame were limited and they would still need a real job someday.

Thanks in part to the Interact Club we held the same accolades for chess club, marching band and drama club members. We saw the best of the best in everybody nerds and all. I the younger sister steered toward more intellectual pursuits. Yes, I was a nerd and at least an honor roll one. My two best friends in high school in my senior year were the 105 pound Carl Hanson and 112 pound Tim Ames wrestlers both of whom were also on the debate team and chess club. Carl also happened to be the best photographer for the yearbook.

Speaking of yearbooks, a good friend wrote in mine when I was a sophomore. He wrote: Leah-- Once upon a time there were two hard-working, beautiful girls. They lived in this huge castle with a swimming pool, a pool table and a big yard that was perfect for playing football, volleyball and anything else you can think of. They had a beautiful mother that made sure that they carried out the orders that the king of the castle set forth for them to do. One day at a basketball game the younger of the two sisters (they were called the strawberry sisters) met this poor dumb peasant and he instantly fell in love with her. They started sitting by each other at the games and really got along well. Then one day both sisters and the peasant and one of his friends went to a party that one of their mutual friends had at his house. They really got along well and found out they had a lot in common. After that they started seeing each other at different places and really having fun. The peasant's friend also got along well with the peasants friend so the two peasants started going over to the castle to see the strawberry sisters and this was good. Then the younger sister's peasant noticed that his friend didn't really treat the older sister too well or at least not as well as she wanted and this wasn't good 'cause she liked him so much that she didn't complain so the peasant decided he would have to change this. He also noticed that he wasn't the only one that was in love with the younger sister, a tall, dark count from another mountain range had entered the picture also. This gave the dumb peasant an idea. Why not try to please the older sister that was being used sort of by the other peasant which wouldn't upset the younger strawberry much because of the count. Anyway the count moved in and so did the dumb peasant and both sisters were satisfied at last and they all lived happily ever after. Who were they? Oh well it was a fun year. I'm glad I met you good luck next year and I'll see you all summer. Love, Bob

Regardless of the paths we would choose to take later on Dad saw to it to be there in the present. He treated all our various collection of friends kindly as he welcomed them to his castle. They, in turn, treated him with the utmost respect. All of our growing up years revolved around us being sheltered. When Pop died Dad threw a conniption fit. Ramee scolded, "What do you mean you are taking the girls to Texas for the funeral? They don't need to see that." Dad took us and I saw my Pop laying in the casket. I remembered a picture of him playing with me. I knew he was dead. Simply put, his salt ran out. Dad had to tell us about death. Dad meant the world to me and I am grateful to him for not sheltering me from seeing what to some was considered traumatic for a child. Our time on earth is finite. Our eternal life is to come. Sheltering us from getting hooked up with the wrong crowd was a must. Sheltering us from seeing death was not an option. His instincts were justified. Now, let us get back to Dating my Daughters.

Dana and I were so happy for our friends to gather. Dad was especially pleased he could oversee it all and keep his girls under close scrutiny. He had a half-court basketball area for the basketballers and a wide open field for any footballers or volleyballers. Everybody loved partying at our house exactly as Dad had planned. Oh, and just so you know the very first time I fell madly in love with Gil was when he affectionately "tackled" me during a flag football game at our house even though he had his eyes set on another girl who I later found out wouldn't give him the time of day.

In the summer we had a pool parties. Everyone respected Dad who loved all forms of competition. One by one these beefy jocks lined up at the diving board. Over and over they entertained Dad with belly flops, cannonballs, twists and tucks. Dad especially loved Gil's dives. He was a slender cross country runner and didn't splash nearly as much as he performed. Dad nicknamed him perfect feet.

Remember the pretty blue mosaic tile border. Dad watched it closely. When it got down to a certain level even though he didn't want to put a damper on all the fun he had to call a halt to the Olympic diving since he knew it would take forever to refill the pool. No one, not one single person objected and respected Dad's wishes.

Another spectacular addition to party central was our rec room. It featured dark wood paneling and a deep gold shag carpet. Raise your right hand now if you remember those trendy 1970's home décor essentials. Once Dad measured and measured again, he went to the store. Not Nichols this time. He went to a billiard table store. He came home with a one inch slate ornate table with woven leather pockets and gold tassel fringe which matched the carpet. We all thought it was extraordinary. He had to hire the help of many strong backs to help him get it in the room. We could tell he seemed conflicted and second guessed himself on such an extravagant purchase. He said it reminded him of one he used to watch his dad play on back in Spur. How sentimental and Dad always worked so hard we thought he deserved a treat. Then he elaborated on his decision. He said I really got a super deal on it. I couldn't pass it up. This table had red felt instead of green. They were practically giving it away. Nice try Dad. Truth be told I believe he went into the store spied the red table, made a beeline for it and wasn't coming home without it even had he had to pay double.

So now we have a fancy eating table and a cement pond. Hey, we are just like *The Beverly Hillbillies*. Sorry I couldn't resist the allegory. Anyway, Dad couldn't resist this new toy not being used for teaching moments. In came pool cues, resin bags, chalk, racks, a pill bottle, crutches, a tiffany style light and billiard balls. We appreciatively studied all these items. Silly us we thought we were just going to start slapping the balls around. Get a new game like Twister, Battleship or Clue. You just start playing and then refer to the instructions once you get stuck. Dad saw fit to pick up a copy of *Minnesota Fats on Pool*. We spent hours learning from Dad the angles, English, and trick shots. We learned the proper way to lag the cue ball just for the sake of seeing who would go first. There was something to this. It is satisfying getting 6 balls into respective pockets in one shot. There were even instructions on how to balance a cue stick so as to hold it properly and just like bowling balls we didn't even know all the sticks were weighted.

We practiced and we learned. Dana and I passed the rigorous tests from the Minnesota Fat's college of knowledge where Dad was the Dean, professor and campus police. Dad's star pupil was my then eight year old brother Johnny. He paid attention. He had quite the knack for this college course. We all kidded him he was so good because he was more at eye level to the balls. He spent hours with Dad practicing trick shots and angles. It is no wonder when we had parties he literally ran the table. Many of the jocks were chagrined when they had to wait to even get a chance to play since they were getting skunked by such a little squirt. Guys were waiting in line to take him on. After being sorely defeated they took their ribbing in stride. Most of his challengers soon tired of being beaten, gave up and went to scope out girls instead.

Yearbook Fairy Tale

DAD AND GIL

The first time Gil got up the gumption to ask me out he pulled up in the driveway on a Norton motorcycle he borrowed from a friend. It was loud. I'm talking can't hear yourself talk loud. I'm talking could hear it coming all the way from Purcellville 6 miles away loud. He asked Dad if he could take me on a motorcycle ride. Dad said sure but not on that one. A very few short days later Gil rode in on his newly purchased maroon Honda 750 and asked Dad again. Dad agreed to let him take me for a spin.

Gil was an apprentice carpenter. Once he showed up at what Dad considered a very inopportune moment. Dad decided the living room fireplace needed an update. He was busy laying bricks on either side and across the top. Unfortunately, Dad had a habit of making mortar a little too soupy. When Gil came in Dad was trying to sure up his project so it would set with two by four props. Dad felt embarrassed to say the least but all Gil said was "I've never seen anyone do it like that before."

Many times Gil would come by and I wouldn't even know he was there. I'm not sure if it was me he liked. What he really liked was Dad's grease pit. They were out in the garage working on Gil's Firebird. Soon they realized Gil was going to need a part. Dad could have offered to let him take our orange Comet to get it, but instead he offered him the use of his Lincoln Continental and threw him the keys ever so matter of factly. Gil and I drove to Courtney's Salvage Yard and I swear I have never seen anyone drive so cautiously. He wouldn't even let me speak or distract him as he was so nervous fearing he'd wreck Dad's car.

Another project Dad had been meaning to get to was to fix the long curving stairway from the living room to the upstairs landing. Dana and I many times pictured floating down those graceful stairs on Dad's arm on our wedding day. When Dad first put in these stairs he made a handrail of sorts. He wasn't the type to waste construction material. He had long expanses of copper tubing left over from doing the plumbing so he used these to make the railing. These tubes were attached to a top wooden rail in the shape of a P. They graduated in length as they descended and the last tube at the bottom was twelve feet long. He bored holes at the top and bottom to fit these tubes in place. They were quite sturdy enough but they had one drawback. They rattled. Copper tubing is not stiff and they wiggled. They especially wiggled and therefore rattled each time three little kids went racing down the stairs. We didn't hold onto the pipes. We extended our arms and rattled each pipe on the way down. We could have chosen not to even touch them but we somehow felt compelled to rattle them. It was like strumming a huge harp. "Quit rattling the rails!" we heard often. We couldn't help it. We knew they rattled and we rattled them for years much to Dad's dismay.

I didn't start dating Gil until I was seventeen so that's about thirteen years of rattling. Dad finally got inspired to fix this problem once and for all. He dismantled the pipes and replaced them with spindles. Knowing how expensive a banister would be he decided to make his own. Since it was a curved staircase he used a series of quarter inch slats seven or eight total laminated together and staggered for sturdiness with the last slat having a decorative molding. He slathered each slat with Elmer's wood glue. This was going to be one sturdy banister. As we were doing the project Dad explained how sturdy it would be. He asked, "Remember the pencils?" Once he showed us a pencil and broke it. Then he added more and more pencils and we tried to break the stack, which of course, we couldn't.

The project was going along splendidly that is until Dad ran out of clamps. One highly important attribute about Elmer's wood glue is its ability to adhere to wood practically forever. Unfortunately, it needs time to set. He knew all the clamps weren't ready to move yet. It didn't take him long to figure out where he could round up some spare clamps. These were Dana my sister, Johnny my brother, Mom and me.

He stationed us at intervals and we clamped the slats together with our hands. That went well for a time until we kids started realizing how long this would take but we dared not let go. Pretty soon our hands started cramping up and we started wishing we hadn't rattled the pipes all those years. This was our penance. This is when Gil showed up. This time Dad did not seem embarrassed. He was relieved. Gil assessed our dilemma immediately pitched in and helped Dad glue and clamp for all he was worth. Up until the time Gil showed up we were starting to see the level of frustration on Dad's face. Once Gil came in Dad must have been thinking, "The Calvary has arrived."

Circular stairs after the clanging stopped.

EPILOGUE

Writing this book has deeply affected me. There were many empty Kleenex boxes left as evidence. Also numerous times I probably snotted up my dear, sweet, wonderful husband's shirt sleeves when I needed a consoling hug. There are many more stories I could relate but for now they will be relegated to memories shared at our family dinner table.

Life, each and every day of it is precious. Dad was my rock on earth. When that earth started to crumble and he fell into an abyss I couldn't fathom, he pulled a huge piece of me in it with him. I was pulled back from that abyss by the loving arms of my husband, my Mom and especially by our Savior Jesus Christ. The calming spirit I feel knowing eternal life awaits through God's grace gives me the strength to keep going no matter what. Dad's salt ran out but not of its own accord. I prefer to think the wicked witch of the west savagely snatched up his hourglass and cruelly hurled it to the cold, hard flagstone floor where it was smashed to smithereens. Either way you look at it the outcome was dealt. Many other people in my life have since touched me deeply. I look for little signs of hope everywhere I go. Without a doubt there are guardian angels here.

Years ago when Gil and I were first starting out and moved to West Virginia we were barely making it. I knew we didn't have money but we had each other and Gil and I made the conscious decision for me to stay home with the kids. Like his father Gilbert Sr. did supporting his brood of five, Gil worked sunup to sundown and then some to support us. My little Sarah was growing like a weed. She was my sunshiny dandelion. Her roots were deep in the ground but I wasn't about to pluck her out as I had done with the dandelions I plucked with Reverend Tracy. One day I simply thought to myself only, "God I wish we could afford a new winter coat for her." The very next day a bag of clothes was on my porch. I have no idea who left it. Smack dab on the top of the bag was a plush velvet red winter coat with white embroidery and a hood with white fur. Sarah loved it and it fit perfectly with room to spare. The rest of the bag was also filled with clothes I hadn't even thought to mention also needing. I was overwhelmed and sat right down and wept and laughed for joy.

It is my hope when you read "Dad Stories" you smiled knowing we may not understand yet how or why stuff happens but God will show us someday. We simply have to wait and trust His will. As my teenage son Stephen used to say, "Peace Out."

Sincerely,
Leah A. Hawkins
a.k.a Nana

Hey John, cement's not too soupy this time?

More cement

Radiant heat

Quite an undertaking

Dad liked using me when measuring the enormity of projects.

Attention to details in the living room

Construction well under way

Just another day on the job for Dad and his helper.

Starting to see the vision

Gramps supervising the world's greatest stonemason beginning the garage foundation.

Ramee and Gramps' Norwegian Elkhound checking out the living room.
He loved finding and tossing blacksnakes around.

Before the renovation

Used to be the milking parlor. Soon to be the kitchen.

Dad loved exposing stone from the barn wherever he could

View from the kitchen wall to the front foyer

All Dad and Mom's skill and hard work was not wasted.

ABOUT THE AUTHOR

L eah or Nana is a mom and grandmother to 4 grandkids Hailey Lynn Barrett, Guinevere Anna Hawkins, Phoenix Orion Hawkins and Brady Raiden Burns. She lives near Harpers Ferry, West Virginia with her loving husband of forty-one years and counting. They were married on April Fool's day. She graduated from Radford University in 1981. She taught French and Spanish, but by a mutual decision she and her husband determined she should resign and take care of their own brood when they were little. Once they reached school age she worked as a store manager, insurance agent and then a security escort and receptionist for Lockheed Martin. She worked for Hobby Lobby in Leesburg, Virginia her dream job. One of her favorite pastimes is crochet. She loved getting yarn extra cheap with her employee discount.

She never has, nor ever will, stop believing in Santa Claus. He represents the "spirit" of giving. She strives to keep the Christmas spirit in her heart all year long. She also steadfastly believes all stuffed animals are endowed with "magical wish". She firmly believes "Stuffies" most fervent hope is to be hugged and loved by a child. One of the greatest joys in life to her is to hug the stuffing out of her own grandkids as well as any other little ones who end up on her lap from time to time.

www.ingramcontent.com/pod-product-compliance
Lightning Source LLC
Chambersburg PA
CBHW051217120626
46547CB00013B/1394